Windows 7 Explained

Books Written by the Same Authors

BP719	Microsoft Office 2010 Explained
BP718	Windows 7 Explained
BP714	An Introduction to Google for the Older Generation
BP710	An Introduction to Windows Live Essentials
BP706	An Introduction to Windows 7
BP703	An Introduction to Windows Vista
BP595	Google Explored
BP590	Microsoft Access 2007 explained
BP585	Microsoft Excel 2007 explained
BP584	Microsoft Word 2007 explained
BP583	Microsoft Office 2007 explained
BP581	Windows Vista explained
BP580	Windows Vista for Beginners
BP569	Microsoft Works 8.0 & Works Suite 2006 explained
BP563	Using Windows XP's Accessories
BP558	Microsoft Works 8.0 & Works Suite 2005 explained
BP557	How Did I Do That ... in Windows XP
BP555	Using PDF Files
BP550	Advanced Guide to Windows XP
BP545	Paint Shop Pro 8 explained
BP538	Windows XP for Beginners
BP525	Controlling Windows XP the easy way
BP514	Windows XP explained
BP509	Microsoft Office XP explained
BP498	Using Visual Basic
BP493	Windows Me explained
BP491	Windows 2000 explained
BP487	Quicken 2000 UK explained
BP341	MS-DOS explained
BP284	Programming in QuickBASIC
BP258	Learning to Program in C

Windows 7 Explained

by

P.R.M. Oliver

and

N. Kantaris

Bernard Babani (publishing) Ltd
The Grampians
Shepherds Bush Road
London W6 7NF
England

www.babanibooks.com

Please Note

Although every care has been taken with the production of this book to ensure that any projects, designs, modifications and/or programs, etc., contained herewith, operate in a correct and safe manner and also that any components specified are normally available in Great Britain, the Publishers and Author(s) do not accept responsibility in any way for the failure (including fault in design) of any project, design, modification or program to work correctly or to cause damage to any equipment that it may be connected to or used in conjunction with, or in respect of any other damage or injury that may be so caused, nor do the Publishers accept responsibility in any way for the failure to obtain specified components.

Notice is also given that if equipment that is still under warranty is modified in any way or used or connected with home-built equipment then that warranty may be void.

British Library Cataloguing in Publication Data:

A catalogue record for this book is available from the British Library

ISBN 978 0 85934 718 1

Cover Design by Gregor Arthur

Printed and bound in Great Britain for
Bernard Babani (publishing) Ltd

Some History

The first version of Windows was produced by Microsoft in 1983 as a graphical extension to its Disc Operating System (MS-DOS).

In 1987, an Intel 386 processor specific version of Windows was launched that was able to run in multiple 'virtual 8086' mode, but Windows applications were unable to use any extended memory above the 1 MB. In 1990, however, Windows version 3.0 solved this problem and became a huge success. Two years later, the much needed update, Windows 3.1, was released to fix most of the program bugs in version 3.0. Windows for Workgroups 3.1, followed in October 1992, and started to give the program the power to control small networked groups of computers. This was strengthened in October 1993 with the 3.11 release, which included 32-bit file management and more networking support.

Then, three years later, came Windows 95, a 32-bit operating system in its own right which made full use of the 32-bit features of the then available range of Intel processor chips. Microsoft had also put a lot of effort into this system to make it compatible with almost all existing Windows and MS-DOS based applications. This meant that parts of Windows 95 were still only 16-bit in operation.

In June 1998, Microsoft launched Windows 98 which ran faster, crashed less frequently, supported a host of new technologies, such as DVD for storing digital video, and improved MMX multimedia. In May 1999 Windows 98 Second Edition was released.

In September 2000, Microsoft released Windows Me, as the direct upgrade to Windows 95/98 for the home PC. Windows Me loaded faster and ran more reliably. In addition, Windows Me incorporated Wizards that let you set up home networks and gave you the ability to share Internet connections, had improved support for digital cameras, video recorders, and multimedia with the introduction of the Windows Media Player 7.

In February 2000, Microsoft released Windows 2000 Professional, together with two additional Windows NT compatible versions of the software; Server and Advanced Server. Users of Windows 95/98 could easily upgrade to the Windows 2000 Professional version of this Operating System (OS), while users of Windows NT could upgrade to one of the other two versions of the OS.

In October 2001, Microsoft released Windows XP (XP for eXPerience) in two flavours; the Home edition (less expensive) as the direct upgrade to Windows 98/Me for home users and the Professional edition (more expensive but with additional functionality) for Windows 2000 or business users. Windows XP looked different to previous versions of Windows – there were changes to the desktop icons, start menu and the Control Panel, while other concepts were borrowed from Windows Me or Windows 2000.

There followed two major updates in the form of Service Pack 1 (SP1) and, in August 2004, Service Pack 2 (SP2). The latter update focused mainly on security of the computer, and was over 260 MB in size. Microsoft made security the central theme of SP2, although there were some additional features that were not specifically geared to protecting your computer.

In February 2007, Microsoft launched Windows Vista with software that allowed you to browse the Web, send and receive e-mails, burn CDs and DVDs, edit photos and videos, and improved home entertainment. It also came with a range of security tools. BUT the hardware industry was slow to produce drivers for Vista and it developed a reputation for not working well with peripheral equipment. The computing and business industries did not convert to it.

In October 2009 Windows 7 was finally released after many months of successful testing by millions of end users. The result is the best operating system so far produced, arguably by anyone. Certainly this is our opinion.

About this Book

Windows 7™

Windows 7 Explained was written for you if you want to quickly explore the workings of Microsoft's new Windows operating system. Windows 7 manages the available resources of your computer and 'controls' the programs that run on it. To get the most from your computer it is important that you have a good working knowledge of Windows 7.

The book is produced in full colour and covers the Windows 7 environment with its many windows, boxes, applications and other controls. Chapters include:

- Introducing the versions of Windows 7 and the methods of installing it on your PC.

- An overview of the stylish new interface, including the Desktop, Taskbar and Aero effects.

- Working with Explorer folders, libraries and files, CDs and DVDs and a few useful things to do.

- How to work with and organise your digital photographs and load them from your camera.

- Using Windows Media Player to store and play your music and other digital media.

- How to generally control your PC, keep it healthy, send faxes and work with application programs.

- Obtaining, installing and using Windows Live Mail for your e-mail needs.

- Using Internet Explorer 8 for your Web browsing.

- Connecting to wireless networks and setting up a HomeGroup or mixed PC network.

- How to use Windows tools to look after and keep your PC and data safe.

- Using mobility tools to keep your laptop PC running and how to use Windows 7's Accessibility features if you have poor eyesight or have problems using the keyboard or mouse.

- An overview of how to find and use the main accessory programs and games packaged with Windows 7.

- An appendix is included listing the main keyboard shortcuts you can use to help make you work faster.

The material in the book is presented using everyday language, avoiding jargon as much as possible. It was written with the non technical, non computer literate person in mind.

We hope that with its help you will be able to get the most out of your computer when using Windows 7, and that you will be able to do it in the shortest, most effective and enjoyable way. Most of all, have fun!

About the Authors

Phil Oliver graduated in Mining Engineering at Camborne School of Mines and has specialised in most aspects of surface mining technology, with a particular emphasis on computer related techniques. He has worked in Guyana, Canada, several Middle Eastern and Central Asian countries, South Africa and the United Kingdom, on such diverse projects as: the planning and management of bauxite, iron, gold and coal mines; rock excavation contracting in the UK; international mining equipment sales and international mine consulting. He later took up a lecturing position at Camborne School of Mines (part of Exeter University) in Surface Mining and Management. He has now retired, to spend more time computing, writing and messing about in boats.

Noel Kantaris graduated in Electrical Engineering at Bristol University and after spending three years in the Electronics Industry in London, took up a Tutorship in Physics at the University of Queensland. Research interests in Ionospheric Physics, led to the degrees of M.E. in Electronics and Ph.D. in Physics. On return to the UK, he took up a Post-Doctoral Research Fellowship in Radio Physics at the University of Leicester, and then a lecturing position in Engineering at the Camborne School of Mines, Cornwall, (part of Exeter University), where he was also the CSM Computing Manager. At present he is IT Director of FFC Ltd.

To Andrew

Who left us suddenly while this book was being planned.

Trademarks

Microsoft, **Windows**, **Windows 7**, **Windows Aero**, **Windows XP**, and **Windows Vista** are either registered trademarks or trademarks of Microsoft Corporation. **Wi-Fi** is a trademark of the Wi-Fi Alliance.

All other brand and product names used in the book are recognised as trademarks, or registered trademarks, of their respective companies.

Contents

1

Windows 7 Introduction

Microsoft have really produced a winning operating system with Windows 7. By the end of July 2010 they reported sales of 175 million licences, making it the fastest selling operating system in history. About half of these sales were with new computers and the rest were installed as upgrades to older systems. We are not surprised with this success. We have both used Windows 7 since the first test versions came out.

Windows 7 not only looks good on your computer but it performs well too. It is both stylish and fast. We have installed it on over 7 different PCs and it has run quickly and efficiently on them all. Sharing data across multiple PCs and mobile devices is easy with Windows 7 using Wi-Fi networks and HomeGroups. Navigation and finding programs and files is a lot easier too, especially the ones you have been recently working with.

Windows 7 is the most secure version of Windows so far, with most of its protection, such as Windows Defender's anti-spyware software and Windows Firewall, taking place unobtrusively in the background. It has built-in support for multi-touch screens, handwriting and voice, but you need suitable hardware to use these features. Unfortunately we don't have it, so we won't mention these again!

Versions

Windows 7 is available in the UK in four main editions, which are true supersets of one another. If you upgrade from one version to the next, you keep all the features and functionality from the previous version

Windows 7 Starter

The lowest-end Windows 7 edition is bundled with low-end computers such as netbooks.

Windows 7 Starter includes the basic Windows 7 user interface, but not Windows Aero, which provides the "glass" windows and Aero Desktop Enhancements such as Aero Peek, Aero Snaps, Aero Shake and Aero Background. It has Windows Search, Action Center, Windows Firewall and User Account Control (UAC), Parental Controls, Windows Backup with system image capabilities (but not network-based backups), Windows Gadgets, Games Explorer with 6 basic games installed (FreeCell, Hearts, Minesweeper, Purble Place, Solitaire, and Spider Solitaire), and a basic set of utilities including Calculator, Paint, Windows Fax and Scan, WordPad, and XP Viewer.

Starter also provides basic digital media functionality, with Windows Media Player, but not Windows Media Center, DVD playback, Windows DVD Maker, or multi-touch. As standard you can't even change the desktop wallpaper!

Windows 7 Home Premium

Most people will be happy with this version. Home Premium builds on Windows 7 Starter's core feature set, adding the Windows Aero user interface (Flip 3D, Live Taskbar Thumbnails, and live icon previews in Explorer). It also provides more fun premium games, such as Internet Backgammon, Internet Checkers, Internet Spades, and Mahjong Titans, and some useful utilities like Snipping Tool, Sticky Notes, and Windows Journal.

With Home Premium you get a more advanced version of Windows Media Player, Windows Media Center, DVD playback capabilities, and Windows DVD Maker.

Using Windows 7 Home Premium, you can create your own HomeGroups, and use PC-to-PC sharing of documents, music, photos, and videos over your home network. It includes Windows Mobility Center, support for the Windows Sideshow gadget technology, and full Tablet PC and multi-touch functionality.

Windows 7 Professional

This version includes business-oriented features like support for Active Directory-based domains, access to Windows XP Mode, automated network backup features to Windows Backup, lets you remotely control one PC from another, and gives Offline Files support, so you can access network-based documents while disconnected from that network.

Windows 7 Ultimate

This version is expensive and includes every single Windows 7 feature. It provides support for the BitLocker and BitLocker To Go drive encryption technologies, and other features well outside the scope of this book, or us, for that matter!

We have used the Windows Home Premium edition to write this book, as most home PC users will find that this version contains all the facilities they will ever need.

For the rest of this chapter we cover what hardware you need to upgrade your computer's operating system from a previous version of Windows to Windows 7, what you need to know prior to installing it, and how to install it whether you choose to upgrade or make a clean install.

If you have bought a computer with Windows 7 already installed, then you could easily skip the rest of the chapter.

System Requirements

Scan your PC for compatibility
Download and run the Windows 7 Upgrade
Advisor. ◉

Fig. 1.1 Downloading the Windows 7 Upgrade Advisor

You can check your PC before you buy Windows 7 by down-loading and running the free **Windows 7 Upgrade Advisor** available at:

www.windows7.com

It will scan your PC and let you know how your PC, devices, and programs will work with Windows 7, including a report detailing any updates you should make before you upgrade.

To run Windows 7 a PC requires at least:

A processor with a speed of 1 GHz or faster 32-bit (x86) or 64-bit (x64), 1 GB (gigabyte) of system memory (RAM) (32-bit) or 2 GB RAM (64-bit), a graphics processor that is DirectX 9 capable with a WDDM 1.0 or higher driver, 16 GB available hard disc space (32-bit) or 20 GB (64-bit).

To use all of Windows 7's features you will also need:

- Internet access.

- Depending on resolution, video playback may require additional memory and advanced graphics hardware.

- For some Windows Media Center functions a TV tuner and additional hardware may be required.

- Windows Touch and Tablet PCs require specific hardware.

- HomeGroup requires a network and PCs running Windows 7.

- DVD/CD authoring requires a compatible optical drive.

- Music and sound require audio output.

Upgrading to Windows 7

Windows 7 is sold as either a 32-bit or a 64-bit Operating System (OS), with discs for both included in the box. To use the 64-bit OS you will require a 64-bit computer, so be careful, most aren't. If you need to find out which you have, check in the **System** section of the **Control Panel**.

You will also have to decide whether to:

- Do an Upgrade – which replaces Windows Vista with Windows 7 and retains all your settings, data files, and programs, or

- Do a Custom installation – after backing-up your settings and data files carry out a clean install. This cures the gradual slowdown that tends to happen to most PCs over time and cleans your PC of any bugs it might have picked up from the Internet. But, the downside is that you'll have to reinstall all your programs. If you are upgrading from Windows XP this is your only option.

Whichever you do it is always a good idea to backup your settings and data files before installing a new operating system. This is quite easy using **Windows Easy Transfer** which transfers files and settings from a computer running Windows XP, Vista, or Windows 7 to another computer (or the same one later) running Windows 7. It does not transfer your programs though, you will have to re-install these.

The Windows Easy Transfer Utility

This is most easily carried out if you have a USB flash drive (memory stick) or an external hard disc.

To start the procedure click the **Start** button 🔵 on the left end of the Taskbar to open the **Start** menu. Type **transfer** in the search box at the bottom, or use the **All Programs**, **Accessories**, **System Tools** menu commands, and click the 🔵 Windows Easy Transfer button. This opens the application as shown in Fig. 1.2 on the next page.

Fig. 1.2 The Easy Transfer Opening Window

Click the **Next** button and choose **An external hard disk or USB flash drive** as the destination to save the Transfer file, as shown here. Click the **Next** button again and select **This is my old computer** from the list.

Windows Easy Transfer then scans for files that can be transferred. Select the ones you want saved during the process and click **Next** again. You will be prompted for an optional password in the next window. Choose where to save your Transfer file and what to name it, then finally click the **Save** button to begin the saving process. This can take some time depending on the overall size of the data being saved.

When you have installed your new copy of Windows 7 you can start the procedure again but this time select **This is my new computer** when asked. Then just follow the instructions to transfer your files and settings to your new system setup.

Installing Windows 7

To save time and help avoid problems during an installation of Windows 7 you should:

• Plug in and switch on all the peripheral devices you will be using with Windows 7.

• Connect to the Internet. This way you will get the latest installation updates, including security and hardware driver updates that can help with the installation.

Upgrade to Windows 7

If you have Windows Vista on your computer you can upgrade to Windows 7, and keep your files, settings, and programs. If you have Windows XP you have to do a Custom Installation so go to the next section.

Turn on your computer so that Windows Vista starts normally and then place the Windows installation disc into your computer's DVD drive. On the Install Windows page, click **Install now**.

If you are connected to the Internet, choose to go online to get the latest updates from the next window, and then accept the licence terms. In the **Which type of installation do you want?** window click Upgrade to begin. If your system has applications installed that are incompatible with Windows 7, or you are trying to do something irregular, you might see a compatibility report at this stage. In this case you should just follow any instructions given.

If all is well you just have to be patient now as this type of installation can take up to a couple of hours, depending on your system. Your PC will reboot a number of times.

You will be asked to input your product key which is usually on a label on the Windows 7 packaging, to configure Automatic Updates, to review your time and date settings (which should already be correct), to select your computer's network location (Home, Work, or Public network), and to configure any HomeGroup sharing. Then you are done.

A Clean Installation

We have found it better to carry out a Custom, or Clean, installation and to let it format the hard disc as well. This way you end up with a much faster and cleaner computer and can see Windows 7 at its best.

We will describe this procedure next, but if you want more detailed information go to the Web page at:

www.microsoft.com/uk/windows

type **installing windows** in the search box, click the Search button 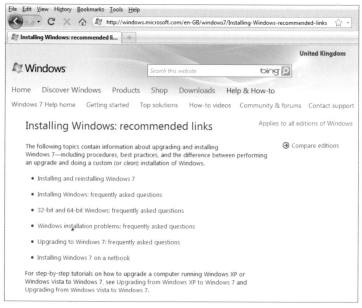 and go to the window shown here.

Fig. 1.3 Getting Online Help with Installing Windows 7

When you choose **Custom** in the **Which type of installation do you want?** window, you install a new copy of Windows on the partition you select. This will erase all your programs and settings. It is essential that you back up any files and settings you want to keep so that you can restore them. You must manually reinstall all your programs though.

To format your hard disc during the Windows 7 installation, you need to start, or boot, your computer using the Windows 7 installation disc. To do this you might have to specify that your computer uses its DVD drive as the first startup device by changing a setting in the computer's basic input/output system (or BIOS).

How to do this varies with different manufacturers. Usually, you press a key (such as **F2** or **F12**) immediately after turning on your computer and before Windows starts, but some PCs display a startup menu. If so just select an option like **BIOS setup**.

When the BIOS setup screen appears in black and white, select the **Boot order option** (or something similar), select the DVD drive as the first startup device, save the setting changes, and then exit the BIOS. This may sound a bit heavy but if you take your time it should be no problem.

Turn on your computer so that Windows starts normally, open the DVD drive and insert the Windows 7 installation disc, then restart your computer. Press a key when prompted to boot the PC from your DVD drive, and then follow the instructions that appear.

On the **Install Windows** page, enter your language and other preferences, and then click **Next** and accept the licence terms. On the **Which type of installation do you want?** page, click Custom.

On the **Where do you want to install Windows?** page, select **Drive options (advanced)**. Select the partition that you want to change, usually C:, and the formatting option you want to perform, and then just follow the instructions to finish installing Windows 7. You will be asked to name your computer and set up an initial user account.

The Windows.old Folder

If you delete or format a partition that contains a version of Windows as described above, all the data on the partition is permanently deleted.

However, if there is an existing copy of Windows on the partition you selected, and you don't format or delete the partition, your user files will be saved to a **Windows.old** folder on the partition, which you can browse after the installation completes.

Don't forget to use the Windows Easy Transfer Utility to transfer your files and settings to your new system setup, as described on page 6.

Once you have restored your files after installing Windows, you can then delete the **Windows.old** folder. It can be important to do this as the amount of data stored in the folder can be very large.

Anti-virus Software

You should now have a running version of Windows 7 to play with, but before you do anything else you should reinstall your anti-virus software. Without it you would be very vulnerable on the Internet.

If you don't have any and you don't want to pay for this you can download excellent free anti-virus and anti-spyware protection at:

http://free.avg.com

We have used this on some of our computers for many years.

2

A First Look at Windows 7

The Windows 7 Desktop

When you switch on your PC and enter your user details,
Windows 7 opens with the Desktop (or working area of the
screen), as shown for our version in Fig. 2.1 below.

Fig. 2.1 A Windows 7 Opening Screen

This new Desktop image for Windows 7 is certainly very
colourful, but whether you want to look at it every day is
another matter. It is very easy to change though, as we cover
later in Chapter 7. Microsoft have provided quite a few
alternative images, and even some UK photographs.

Notice the completely new **Taskbar** at the bottom of the
screen. Some of its new features take a little getting used to,
but take it from us, it is worth the effort.

The Taskbar

By default, the **Taskbar** is located at the bottom of the Windows 7 Desktop, but as long as it is not locked (if necessary right-click the **Taskbar** and uncheck the **Lock the Taskbar** option), you can 'drag' it to any border of the screen. In fact with a widescreen monitor the **Taskbar** works very well vertically on the right side of the Desktop.

The **Taskbar** is the area of the Desktop that contains the **Start** button ⊕ on the left, the **Notification Area** and the **Show Desktop** button ∥ on the right, and buttons for all your pinned and open programs, as shown in Fig. 2.2.

Fig. 2.2 The Windows 7 Taskbar

As with previous versions of Windows, when you open a program or window, a button for it is placed on the **Taskbar**. But Windows 7 has no Quick Launch toolbar, you add (or pin) shortcuts straight onto the Taskbar itself.

Fig. 2.3 Windows 7 Taskbar Buttons

So the applications you use most can always be shown on the **Taskbar**, whether they are open or not. Running programs and open windows are shown by buttons with a visible border, whereas 'pinned' shortcuts that are not open, such as Media Player in Fig. 2.3 above, have no borders.

If an item is not open, just clicking its button will open it. You can preview the contents of an open application by hovering the mouse pointer over its button on the **Taskbar**. A thumbnail appears showing a miniature version of the window, which even works if the window has a video or animation playing.

In Fig. 2.4 on the next page, we show the preview of what was open in our Internet Explorer at the time.

Fig. 2.4 Thumbnails Showing Open Explorer Tabs

As you can see, there were three tabs open and each is shown as a thumbnail. Moving the mouse pointer over a thumbnail temporarily displays that window full size on the screen so you can see in more detail what it contains – this is called Aero Peek. Clicking a thumbnail will open the program with that view active, and clicking the Close button ⊠ on a thumbnail will close that tab or window. Moving the mouse pointer away will stop the operation with everything left the same.

So now, using the **Taskbar**, you can always see what applications you have open, which is the active one, what it contains, and quickly switch between them.

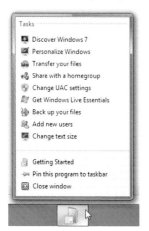

Fig. 2.5 A Windows 7
Jump List

When the **Taskbar** is unlocked you can now drag your **Taskbar** buttons and place them in your preferred order.

If you right-click a **Taskbar** button, a new **Jump List** appears with a list of pre-programmed, or common, actions associated with the clicked object.

In Fig. 2.5 we show this for the Getting Started window, which can be opened from the **Start** menu (Fig. 2.6). The programmed actions associated with the button are shown as **Tasks** at the top of the list. Those at the bottom are available for all program and window buttons, and are all you will see for most applications not specially written with this Windows 7 feature in mind.

The **Pin this program to the taskbar** option is one way to place a shortcut to a program 'permanently' on the **Taskbar**. Another way is to right-click a program or shortcut in the **Start** menu and select the **Pin to Taskbar** option from the context menu that opens (see Fig. 2.15, on page 22).

The Start Button and Menu

 Windows 7 should start up as soon as you switch on your PC, so you don't have to start it manually. Then, clicking the **Start** button 🔵 on the left end of the Taskbar, or pressing the Windows key 🏴, opens the **Start** menu which gives you access to all the applications and settings on your computer. Fig. 2.6 shows a typical **Start** menu, as well as the **Recycle Bin** icon.

Fig. 2.6 The Opening Windows 7 Start Menu with Large Icons

Once you start using Windows 7, the menu in the left pane will have two parts (Fig. 2.7 below). When first used, as shown in Fig. 2.6, Windows 7 places some useful shortcuts on it. As you use Windows it will automatically replace these with shortcuts to the applications you use most frequently. You can also add (or pin) shortcuts to your most frequently used programs to the top section of the menu. So this section will change as you use your PC.

In the pane on the right are shortcuts to Documents, Pictures, Music, Games, Computer, Control Panel, etc., which are normally common to all users.

Just one left-click with your mouse on any of the shortcuts on the **Start** menu will open the application or process.

Fig. 2.7 Start Menu (Small Icons) with a Jump List Open

The Windows 7 **Start** menu also supports the **Jump Lists** that we saw earlier. As shown in Fig. 2.7 above, the list appears on the right side of the **Start** menu. According to Microsoft, the new **Start** menu is also touch-friendly, but we don't have the hardware to check this out.

The Notification Area

This is the area, also called the **System Tray**, on the right of the Taskbar that includes a digital clock and date, as well as icons showing the status of the Action Center , power (for a laptop), network (ethernet) or (wireless), and the volume setting of your speakers . Other application icons are hidden by default and their notifications are suppressed.

When you click an icon, an information bubble opens showing the status for that setting. Clicking the **Network** icon , or , for instance, displays information about whether you are connected to a network, as shown in Fig. 2.8.

Fig. 2.8 Network Icon

Try clicking the **Volume** icon to open the volume controls so you can control the loudness of the speakers attached to your PC, or built into your laptop.

Clicking the **Action Center** icon (new to Windows 7) gives you a quick view of the status of your PC, as shown in Fig. 2.9. If any problems are shown, you can click the **Open Action Center** link to find out what they are and hopefully how you can solve them.

Fig. 2.9 The Action Center

By default, Windows 7 places any other icons in a 'hidden' area, but you can click the **Show hidden icons** button to temporarily show them again (Fig. 2.10).

If you don't like this default arrangement you can click the **Customize** link and select which icons and notifications appear on your **Taskbar**.

Fig. 2.10

The Show Desktop Button

The **Show desktop** button █ is now on the right-hand end of the **Taskbar** and has two functions. Hovering your pointer over it temporarily closes all your open windows and lets you see any gadgets or icons you have on your Desktop – this is called Aero Peek. When clicked it acts as the **Show desktop** button and minimises all open windows to the **Taskbar**. Clicking it again re-opens the same windows.

Windows Aero

As it did with Vista, 'Windows Aero' gives a strong visual experience to Windows 7. If your PC is capable of 3D graphics you should be able to see and use the new window colours, themes and transparent borders, and get the **Flip 3D** feature, shown in Fig. 2.11, when you hold the 🏁 Windows key down and press the **Tab** key. Every time you press the **Tab** key, or rotate the scroll wheel on your mouse, the windows on the screen change position in really spectacular fashion. To open a particular window, release the 🏁 key when it comes to the front.

Fig. 2.11 Flip 3D in Action

Another way to quickly identify and open the window you want is to use the **Alt+Tab** keys together. This lets you flip through thumbnails of your windows by keeping the **Alt** key depressed and pressing the **Tab** key repeatedly. If you pause on a thumbnail you get an Aero Peek view of its window in the background. Releasing the **Alt** key opens the selected window.

Aero also includes some new features for window management, that don't use the standard window controls, which with higher and higher resolution displays are getting smaller and harder to use.

Aero Shake

Windows 7 includes a unique new way, called **Aero Shake**, to minimise all windows except for the one currently active. You just grab it by the title bar and 'shake vigorously'. This does not always work with older programs. Shaking again will restore the other windows.

Aero Snaps

By dragging open windows in certain ways, you can 'snap' them to the edges of the screen, and maximise, or minimise them. These methods do not work on 'full size' windows.

To **maximise** the current window, drag its title bar up toward the top of the screen. When the cursor touches the top of the screen, the window will maximise.

To **'snap' the current window to the left side** of the screen, drag it to the left. When the cursor hits the left side of the screen, the window will snap to that edge and resize to occupy the left half of the screen (see also Fig. 3.9, page 34).

To **snap to the right side** of the screen, drag the window to the right. When the cursor hits the screen edge, the window will resize and snap to the right half of the screen. These can be used together. If you snap one window to the left and one to the right, you can very easily drag and drop files between them.

These features may not work with Windows 7 Starter.

It is very easy to control Aero and Windows 7's other visual features by right-clicking on an empty part of the Desktop and selecting the **Personalize** option from the context menu. This opens the window shown in Fig. 7.7 on page 102, in which you can customise most of Windows 7's features. You can spend many happy hours here! Clicking on **Window Color**, opens the very colourful window shown in Fig. 7.10 for you to play with. You can control the colours of your windows and set whether they are 'transparent' or not. These settings will be altered, though, whenever you select a new **Theme**.

User Accounts

Windows 7 makes it possible for several people to share a computer (a family maybe) with each having their own set-up. This is done using individual User Accounts. Each account tells Windows 7 what files and folders the holder can access, what changes he or she can make to the computer, and controls personal preferences, such as Desktop backgrounds and colour schemes.

At the top of the **Start** menu the name of the current user is displayed with a picture or icon above it, as shown here and in Fig. 2.6. Left-clicking this icon opens the User Accounts window shown in Fig. 2.12.

Fig. 2.12 The User Accounts Window

This is where the person logged on can create or change their user password, choose a different picture or icon, change the name or type of their account, etc.

Running Programs

As Windows 7 is an operating system, it manages the other programs you run on your PC, such as word processors, spreadsheets, databases and games. You can double-click a shortcut icon on your Desktop to open a program, but the **Start** menu (Fig. 2.6) is the main way to access your computer's programs, folders, and settings. As we saw on page 14, clicking the **Start** button on the left end of the Taskbar, opens the **Start** menu. To open a program shown in the left pane of this menu, just click it. The program opens and the **Start** menu closes.

If the program you want isn't listed but you know its name, just start typing the name into the **Search programs and files** box at the bottom of the left pane.

In Fig. 2.13, to open the Notepad text editor, we started typing its name in the **Search** box. The **Start** menu pane instantly displayed search results, right from the first letter typed, and became more selective as each new letter was added.

Fig. 2.13 Searching for a Program

What we were looking for soon appeared at the top of the list under the **Programs** heading. Clicking it opened the Notepad program and closed the **Start** menu.

If all else fails, click **All Programs** above the **Search** box and the left pane will show a long list of programs in alphabetical order, followed by a list of folders, as shown here in Fig. 2.14.

This shows some of the contents of the **All Programs** list on one of our computers, and the contents of the Windows **Accessories** folder.

As with Vista, in Windows 7, programs are given distinctive icons in these lists. Clicking on the **Notepad** option, starts the program in its own window.

Folders, like the **Accessories** folder, have a different icon and can contain other folders, documents, programs or other items.

Fig. 2.14 The All Programs List with the Accessories Folder Opened

To close an opened folder on this list, left-click it again. To get back to the programs you saw when you first opened the **Start** menu, click **Back** at the bottom of the menu (Fig. 2.14).

Changing the Start Menu

As mentioned earlier, the **Start** menu has the ability to adapt the first of its two-column menus to the way you use your PC. It keeps track of what features and programs you use the most and adds them to the list at the bottom of the left column. For example, if you use **WordPad** a couple of times by selecting it from the **Accessories** sub-menu, next time you click the **Start** button you will see this application pinned to the bottom half of the **Start** menu.

Fig. 2.15 Using a Context Menu

This saves time as you don't then have to scroll through menu lists to find the application you want to use.

To remove an application from the left pane of the **Start** menu, right-click it with your mouse and select the option **Remove from this list** from the context menu, as shown in Fig. 2.15. This removes the name of the application from the list, but not the application itself from your hard disc.

You also have the menu options, **Pin to Start Menu** and **Pin to Taskbar**. The first of these adds the program to the top half of the left pane of the **Start** menu which is a more permanent list. The second option pins the selected program to the **Taskbar**, so from then on you will be able to click its button on the **Taskbar** to start the program.

When some programs are installed on your PC they place a shortcut icon on your Desktop, like that shown here. Right-clicking this, displays similar options to those above, so you can pin the program to either the **Start** menu or the **Taskbar**.

Windows 7 does not place shortcut icons on the lower **Start** menu for programs you have pinned on the **Taskbar**, no matter how many times you use the programs.

As with most things in Windows 7 you can customise the **Start** menu and the **Taskbar** by right-clicking on the **Start** button and selecting **Properties**. We will leave it to you to explore the options here. The **Customize** button is a good place to start. This is where we changed the size of the **Start** menu icons shown earlier in Figs 2.6 and 2.7.

Ending a PC Session

Fig. 2.16 Shut Down Options

When you have finished for the day, it is important to save your work and 'turn off' your computer properly, both to protect your data and to save energy. With Windows 7 there are several options for ending the session, all available from the **Power** button at the bottom of the **Start** menu as shown in Fig. 2.16. Clicking the **Start** button 🌐 and hovering the pointer over the right arrow button ▶, will open the options menu shown.

From here you can select to **Switch User**, **Log Off** the current user and leave the computer running so another user can log on, **Lock** the Computer so that it needs a password before you can carry on working, **Restart** the computer to clear the memory settings and reset Windows, put the PC in **Sleep** mode, or use **Hibernate** if the option is available.

By default, the **Shut Down** button ▭Shut Down▭ closes the computer completely, but you can change this by right-clicking the **Start** button 🌐 and selecting **Properties**. If there are updates to install, the **Shut Down** button changes to ▭ Shut Down▭. When you click it in this form, Windows 7 installs the updates and then shuts down the PC.

In sleep mode the display turns off, the computer's fan usually stops and a light on the outside of the case blinks to indicate that the computer is asleep. The whole process takes only a few seconds. When you turn back on again and enter your password, the screen will look exactly as it did when you turned off. Because you don't have to wait for Windows to start, your computer wakes within seconds and you can resume work almost immediately.

If you are a mobile PC user you usually just have to close the lid to put it to sleep, unless you leave your laptop where it could be stolen. In which case it is much safer to shut down completely, so that it does not produce any detectable signal.

Hibernation is a power-saving state designed primarily for laptops. While sleep puts your work and settings in memory and draws a small amount of power, hibernation saves your open documents and programs on your hard disc, and then turns off your computer. This uses the least amount of power, but takes longer to re-start again.

In our experience, sleep and hibernation modes often don't seem to work correctly. If this happens on your PC we suggest you go to the Web site:

www.sevenforums.com/tutorials

and click the **Power Management** icon. Good luck, we have solved many of our Power problems here, and more solutions are added all the time.

3

The Windows 7 Environment

In Windows 7 every user starts with a set of data folders
called simply **My Documents**, **My Pictures**, **My Music** and
My Videos stored in **Libraries**. To see your Libraries, click
the **Start** button , then click your log-on name at the top of
the **Start** menu (see Fig. 2.6) and click **Libraries** in the left
pane. This opens an Explorer window similar to Fig. 3.1
below.

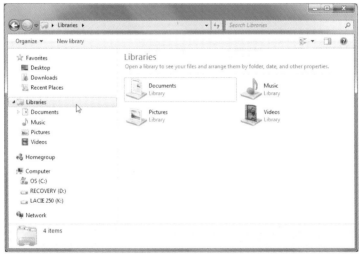

Fig. 3.1 A Set of Personal Libraries

Libraries (see page 38) are new to Windows 7. Although not
folders themselves, they can point to different folders on your
hard disc, or on an external drive attached to your computer.
They let you quickly access files from multiple folders without
moving them from their original location. Say you have music
files on your hard disc and on an external drive, you can now
access all of your music files from the Music library.

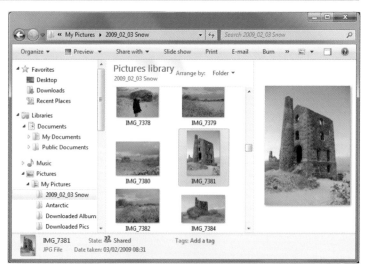

Fig. 3.2 A Folder of Photos in My Pictures

The left pane of the Explorer window, called the **Navigation** pane, lists your **Favorites** and gives you access to tree views of your **Libraries**, your **Computer** and your **Networks**. The right pane lists the folders and files in the selected location.

Clicking a link in the **Navigation** pane opens the contents of that folder in the right pane. Double-clicking a folder in the right pane will open it and display its contents.

In the **Navigation** pane of Fig. 3.2 you can see that the default contents of the **Documents Library** are **My Documents** (your personal documents folder) and **Public Documents** (those available to anyone that uses the computer).

In Fig. 3.2 above, we have clicked on a folder name in the **My Pictures** listing to open it. The photographs in the folder are shown in the centre pane. The right **Preview** pane is opened and closed by clicking the **Preview Pane** button on the toolbar at the top of the window. This shows a larger preview image of whatever is selected in the centre pane.

Parts of a Window

In Fig. 3.3 below we show a typical Windows 7 Explorer window with its constituent parts labelled and later described. By default, menus are not shown in these windows. To see the **Menu** bar in a Windows 7 window, press the **Alt** key, or click the **Organize** button and select **Layout, Menu Bar**.

You may have noticed by now that the buttons on the toolbars of the different Explorer windows change to reflect the type of work you can do in that type of window.

Pictures windows, for example, have a **Slide Show** button, whereas **Music** windows have **Play** and **Play All** buttons.

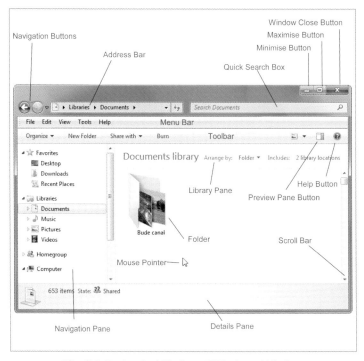

Fig. 3.3 Parts of a Windows 7 Explorer Window

The typical Explorer window is subdivided into several areas which have the following functions:

Area	*Function*
Minimise button	Left-clicking the **Minimise** button stores a window and its contents as an icon on the **Taskbar**. Clicking on such an icon will restore the window.
Maximise button	Left-clicking the **Maximise** button fills the screen with the active window. When that happens, the **Maximise** button changes to a **Restore Down** button which can be used to restore the window to its former size.
Close button	The extreme top right button that you click to close a window.
Navigation buttons 	The **Go Back** (left) button takes you to the previous display, while the **Go Forward** (right) button takes you to the next display. The down-arrow ⬇ gives access to **Recent Pages**.
Address bar 	Shows the location of the current folder. You can change locations here, or switch to an Internet Explorer window by typing a Web address (URL).
Quick search box	The box in which you type your search criteria. As you start typing the first few letters, the displayed files filter down to just the matching terms. This makes finding your files much easier.
Menu bar	The bar which only displays if you press the **Alt** key. It allows you to choose from several menu options. Clicking on a menu item displays the pull-down menu associated with it.

Toolbar

A bar of icons that you click to carry out some common actions. The icons displayed on the toolbar depend on the type of window.

Scroll bars/buttons

The bars/buttons at the extreme right and bottom of each window (or pane within a window) that contain a scroll box/button. Clicking on these allows you to see parts of a document that might not be visible in that size window.

Mouse pointer

The arrow which appears when the pointer is placed over menus, scroll bars, buttons, and folder lists.

Window Panes

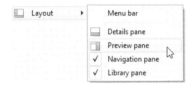

Fig. 3.4 Controlling Panes

With Windows 7's Explorer windows you can control which panes are open by clicking the **Organize** toolbar button, selecting **Layout** from the drop-down menu, and clicking one of the options as shown in Fig. 3.4.

Option	*Function*
Details Pane	To display information on an item.
Preview Pane	To preview the contents of a selected file without opening it.
Navigation Pane	Shows links and folders so that you can easily navigate around your PC.
Library Pane	To manage the contents and view of the Library being looked at.

Menu Bar Options

Each window's menu bar option has associated with it a pull-down sub-menu (you can open the menu by pressing the **Alt** key). To activate a menu or sub-menu option, highlight it by pointing to it, and click the left mouse button.

Items on the sub-menu marked with an arrow to their right ▶, open up additional options when selected.

Most Windows 7 system applications offer the **File**, **Edit**, **View**, **Tools** and **Help** menu options.

Fig. 3.5 A Typical Windows 7 Sub-menu

Note: Having activated a menu, whether from the menu bar or a right-click, you can close it without taking any further action by simply left-clicking the mouse pointer somewhere else on the screen, or by pressing the **Esc** key.

Dialogue Boxes

Three periods after a sub-menu option or command, means that a dialogue box will open when the option or command is selected. A dialogue box is used for the insertion of additional information.

To see a dialogue box, click the **Start** button and select the **Computer** menu option. If necessary, press the **Alt** key to display the **Menu bar**, click **Tools** and on the drop-down sub-menu select **Folder options**. This opens the Folder Options dialogue box with its General tab selected. In Fig. 3.6 on the next page we show this dialogue box with its View tab selected so that you can see different types of option lists.

Fig. 3.6 The Folder Options Dialogue Box

When a dialogue box opens, you can use the **Tab** key to move the dotted rectangle, or focus, from one field to another, or more easily, you can use the mouse.

Some dialogue boxes contain List boxes which show a column of available choices. If there are more choices than can be seen in the area provided, use the scroll bars to reveal them, as above.

Dialogue boxes may contain Check boxes ☑, which offer a list of features you can switch on or off. Selected options show a tick in the box against the option name.

Another feature available is the Option, or Radio button ◉, with a list of mutually exclusive items. The default choice is marked with a blue dot. Unavailable options are dimmed.

To cancel a dialogue box, either press the **Cancel** button, or the **Esc** key enough times to close the dialogue box and then the menu system.

Changing the Date and Time

Fig. 3.7 Date and Time
Properties Dialogue Box

On the far right of the **Taskbar** is a digital clock showing the current time as given by the internal clock of your PC. Left-clicking the time display, opens the pop-up window shown in Fig. 3.7. Clicking the **Change date and time settings** link on this opens the **Date and Time** box, so that you can control your clock.

As you can see here, the clock changes automatically between Summer and Winter times.

On the Internet Time tab you can set your clock to synchronise with an Internet time server, so it should always be correct.

On the Additional Clocks tab, you can set to show up to two extra clocks for

Fig. 3.8 The Date and Time Box

different time zones. With a son in Australia, we find this a useful feature. You can view the extra clocks by hovering the pointer over the normal **Taskbar** clock, as shown here. If you click on the **Taskbar** clock, a pop-up window similar to that in Fig. 3.7 opens, but showing all your clocks.

Manipulating Windows

To use any Windows program effectively, you need to be able to work with a series of windows, and make a window active, move it, or re-size it so that you can see all of it.

Changing the active window – If you have several windows open on the screen, you can make one active by simply clicking it with the left mouse button, or, if it is not visible, click its icon on the **Taskbar**.

Moving a window – To move a window (or a dialogue box), point to its title bar with the mouse, and drag it with the left button depressed until it is where you want on the screen, then release the mouse button. You can only do this if the window does not occupy the full screen and it has a maximise button 🔲 visible.

Minimising and maximising windows – To minimise a window into a **Taskbar** icon, maybe to free up Desktop space, left-click the **Minimize** button 🔲 in the upper-right corner of the window.

To maximise a window so that it fills the entire screen, left-click the **Maximize** button 🔲, or double-click in the title bar. Double-clicking again will restore it.

A window that has been minimised or maximised can be returned to its original size and position on the screen by either clicking on its **Taskbar** icon to expand it to a window, or clicking on the **Restore Down** button 🔲 of a maximised window, to reduce it to its former size.

Re-sizing a window – You can change the size of a window with the mouse by first moving the window so that the side you want to change is visible, then placing the mouse pointer on the edge of the window, or on a corner, so that it changes to a two-headed arrow, then dragging this arrow to get the size you want.

Closing a window – Any window can be closed at any time, to save screen space and memory, by left-clicking its **Close** button 🔲.

New Aero Features

Windows 7 also includes some new ways to manipulate windows. These were developed to take advantage of its new Touch features, which if you have touch-sensitive hardware lets you manipulate the screen with your fingers.

Aero Shake lets you minimise all windows except for the one currently active. You just grab the title bar (keeping the left mouse button depressed) and 'shake vigorously' to minimise all the other open windows.

Aero Snaps let you 'snap' windows to the edges of the screen, and maximise, or minimise them. To **maximise** the current window, you drag its title bar up towards the top of the screen. When the cursor touches the top of the screen, the window will maximise.

To **'snap' the current window to the left side** of the screen, drag it to the left. When the cursor hits the left side of the screen, the window will snap to that edge and resize to occupy the left half of the screen.

Fig. 3.9 In the Process of Snapping a Window to the Left

Fig. 3.9 shows the procedure just before the mouse pointer is released. The gold outline of where the snapped window will go is shown against a very colourful Desktop image.

To **snap to the right side** of the screen, drag the window to the right. When the cursor hits the screen edge and the mouse button is released, the window will resize and snap to the right half of the screen. These can be used together. If you snap one window to the left and one to the right, you can very easily drag and drop files between them.

To **restore** a maximised or snapped window, simply drag it back towards the centre of the screen and it will return to its previous size and position.

When you get used to these new features, they make working with your different application windows a pleasure. To start with though, it can be somewhat disconcerting when a window disappears or suddenly 'takes off on its own'.

Aero Snap is turned on by default in Windows 7, but it is easy to turn it off. To do this, open the **Ease of Access Center** with the ⊞**+U** keyboard shortcut, click the **Make the mouse easier to use** link, and check **Prevent windows from being automatically arranged when moved to the edge of the screen**. Unchecking will turn it on again.

Fig. 3.10 Turning Off the Aero Snap Feature

Help with Windows 7

Whatever you are doing in Windows 7, help is not very far away. Just click the **Start** button 🪟, then click the **Help and Support** menu option to open the main Help window, shown in Fig. 3.11 on the next page.

The **Search Help** text box gives you access to a very powerful Help search facility. Type the word or phrase you want help with into the text box and click the **Search Help** button 🔍. Try it, it's one of our favourite methods.

Fig. 3.11 Windows Help and Support

You can click one of the options in the **Not sure where to start?** section, or use the **Browse Help** button ▋ to open a browsable list.

When you are in a Windows 7 Explorer window, you can also click the **Get Help** button ⊚ on the toolbar, to get specific help on the type of window you are working with.

As long as you are online, you should make sure the **Online Help** button ⊙ Online Help ▾ is showing at the bottom of the **Help** window. This will ensure you have access to Windows 7's latest Help content. It is a new operating system and Microsoft are updating Help quite frequently.

4

Libraries, Folders and Files

On a computer, a **file** contains related information, such as a word-processed letter, a spreadsheet, a digital photo, a video, or a music track. Windows 7 represents files with icons in its Explorer windows, as shown in Fig. 4.1, so you can tell what kind of file an icon represents just by looking at it.

| Text File | Photo | Word File | Excel File | Video |

Fig. 4.1 File Icons in a Documents Window

You control the size of the icons in the window's **View** sub-menu (page 39). Fig. 4.1 above, shows **Large Icons**.

A **folder** is just a container in which you can store files or other folders. Arranging files into logical groups in folders makes it easier to locate and work with them.

Fig. 4.2 Folders in a My Documents Window

By default, Windows 7 provides four special folders for each user, called **My Documents**, **My Pictures**, **My Music**, and **My Videos** stored in the **C:\Users\Username** folder, as shown in Fig. 4.3 for the 'Username' Phil.

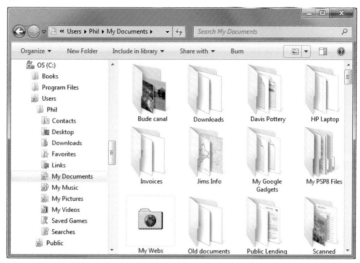

Fig. 4.3 The Default User Folder Structure

Libraries

In Windows 7 you can still open and use these special folders, but now the best way to access the files stored in them is from one of the libraries (see page 25), all of which can be accessed from the **Start** menu. Each Library has a default location to store saved files. In the **Documents** Library, for example, it is the **My Documents** folder. We

recommend that you carry on with this structure, so that photos and folders created for photos would go in the **My Pictures** folder, word processor and spreadsheet files and folders would go in the **My Documents** folder, etc.

In this way, when you click the **Start** button 🏁, the Libraries will be available for you on the top-right of the **Start** menu, as shown here.

You can change how your file and folder icons appear in Windows 7's Explorer windows with the **Views** 'slider' menu on the toolbar of every folder, shown open in Fig. 4.4 below.

Open the folder you want to change. Click the down-arrow next to the **Views** button on the toolbar and move the slider to change the appearance of the icons.

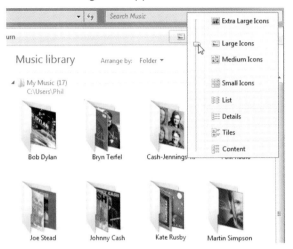

Fig. 4.4 Changing the Size of File and Folder Icons

As shown above, the slider has eight rest positions between **Content** (a new option) and **Extra Large Icons**. You can fine-tune the size of the icons by moving the slider to any point between these positions. As you do this, keep your eye on the **Views** button itself. It changes to show the currently selected view. Very neat.

The Library Pane (see page 29) in each Library window has two controls. The **Includes**: setting lets you manage the locations included in the Library. Clicking the blue link to the right opens the **Library Locations** box in which you can add and remove folders to or from the Library, and change the **Default save location**.

The **Arrange by:** setting lets you filter all the files in the Library and arrange them in various ways, as shown in Fig. 4.5. These vary depending on the type of Library.

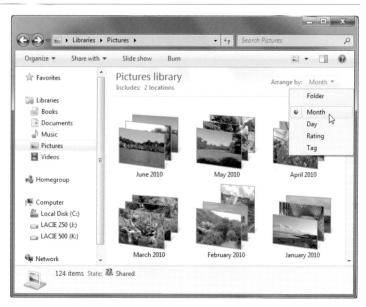

Fig. 4.5 Arranging the Library Contents

Creating a New Library

As well as the four default libraries (Documents, Music, Pictures, and Videos) you can also create new libraries to group together other file collections. In Fig. 4.5 above, for instance, we show a **Books** library we use for our writing work files.

To create a new library first open your personal folder by clicking the **Start** button , click your user name (Phil in our case), and then, in the left pane, click **Libraries** to open the Libraries window as shown in Fig. 4.6 on the next page. Click the **New library** button on the toolbar, type a name for the library, and then press **Enter**.

To copy, move, or save files to the new library, you first put a folder in it so that the library knows where to store the files. This folder then becomes the default save location for the library.

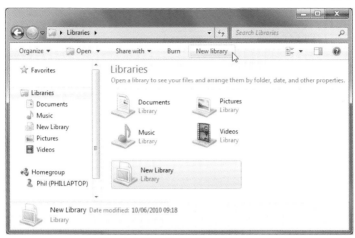

Fig. 4.6 Creating a New Library

To include a folder from your computer in a library click the Windows Explorer button [image] on the Taskbar, select the folder you want to include in the Navigation Pane of the Explorer window, and click the **Include in library** button on the toolbar. Then select the library you want to add to.

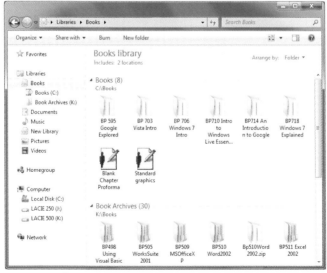

Fig. 4.7 A Library Looking in 2 Locations

Navigation

There are two main ways of navigating through the libraries, folders and files on your computer and any networks attached to it.

The Navigation Pane

You can use the Navigation Pane (Fig. 4.8) to visually see the Libraries and folders on your system. Clicking on an item opens its sub-folders and files in the right-hand pane of the Explorer window. You can also move or copy items directly to a destination in the Navigation Pane.

If your Explorer windows don't have a Navigation Pane on their left side just click the **Organize** button, hover the pointer over **Layout**, and then click **Navigation pane** to display it.

Fig. 4.8 A Typical Navigation Pane

The Address Bar

The Address Bar, also called the "Breadcrumb Bar", appears at the top of every Windows 7 folder window and displays your current location as a series of links separated by drop-down arrows ▶.

Fig. 4.9 The Windows 7 Address Bar

To navigate to a sub-folder in the hierarchy you click the small arrow ▶ to the right of an item in the bar and select from the drop-down menu of its sub-folders. Clicking the arrow ▶ to the left of an item gives access to folders of the same level.

As you can see below, a drop-down menu appears, showing you all the folders (in this case, Libraries) that are available. You can click any of these to navigate there immediately.

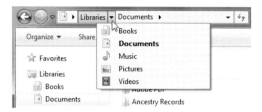

Fig. 4.10 Navigating with the Address Bar

If you click the icon on the left end of the Address Bar (in Fig. 4.11 below) the breadcrumb bar changes and gives the full path of the current folder as shown in Fig. 4.11.

Fig. 4.11 Using Full Address Paths in an Explorer Window

The path is selected so you can copy it to use elsewhere, or type a new path to select another folder (or Internet) location to make active. If you are used to working with 'old style' full path addresses, and many of us are, this will be for you.

For some common Windows 7 locations you can just type their name (such as Videos) straight into the Address Bar and then press **Enter**. This works for: Computer, Contacts, Control Panel, Documents, Favorites, Games, Music, Pictures, Recycle Bin and Videos.

You can also drag the icon on the left end of the Address Bar to create a shortcut, or link to the current location, and drop it in a folder or on the Desktop, as shown in Fig. 4.11.

To return to the usual breadcrumb bar, just click anywhere else in the window.

Fig. 4.12

To the left of the Address Bar the **Back** button takes you to the previous location, while the **Forward** button takes you to the next one of a previously visited sequence.

The down-arrow ▼ of the **Recent Pages** button to the right of these buttons gives access to a drop-down list of the locations you have visited (Fig. 4.12).

So there you have it! The Address Bar lets you navigate to any folder on your hard disc or network and gives a much better view of the folder's contents. If you have previously used Windows Vista the changes are only a slight improvement. But Windows XP users will probably take longer to come to terms with this new navigation bar.

Creating a New Folder

To create a new folder in a Library or other folder, open the folder you want it to be in, and left-click the **New Folder** toolbar button.

When Windows 7 creates a new folder it gives it the very original name **New Folder**, places it alphabetically in the list of existing items, and highlights the name ready for you to rename it, as shown here. You just type a new name for the folder.

Perhaps an easier way to create a new folder is to go to the location, or folder, where you want to create it, right-click a blank area in the window, select **New**, **Folder** from the context menu, type a name for the new folder, and press **Enter**. This is the way we usually do it.

To rename a file or folder, first select it, then left-click in the name area to select the old name and just type the new name.

Searching for Files and Folders

Windows 7 has a facility to instantly **Search programs and files** on your computer. This appears on the **Start** menu, immediately above the **Start** button , and in every Explorer type window. To locate programs, files, e-mail messages and other items on your PC just type a file name, a property, or some of the text in a file, and **Search** should quickly find and open it for you.

To find a specific file or folder located anywhere on your PC, open the **Start** menu and start typing in the **Search programs and files** box. As you type, the pane instantly displays search results, right from the first letter typed, with the list becoming more selective as each new letter is added. The results are listed in categories as shown in our example in Fig. 4.13.

If the file or folder you want is listed, simply click it to open it.

If not, you can click the **See more results** link at the bottom of the list, to open the search in a Search Folder as shown in Fig. 4.14, on the next page.

Fig. 4.13 Searching for Files

With Windows 7 you can use the **Save search** button on the toolbar to save the search criteria you have used together with the search results in the **Searches** folder in your Users section (as shown in Fig. 4.3 on page 38). Double-clicking this saved search in the future, will start a new search of the same type.

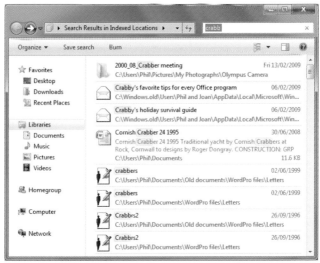

Fig. 4.14 Results in a Search Folder

If you know what folder a file is in, you can open it and use the **Quick Search** box in the folder window to carry out your search in the same way.

Working with Files and Folders

The longer you work with a computer the more files and folders you accumulate. To keep things manageable you need at least to be able to copy, move and delete them.

Selecting Files and Folders – In Windows you have to select an item before you can do something with it. When it is selected in Windows 7, a file or folder is given a pale blue surround, as shown in Fig. 4.15 on the facing page.

To select one file or folder in a window just click it. To select several you have three main options:

- If they form a contiguous list, left-click the first in the list, then with the **Shift** key depressed, click the last in the list.

Fig. 4.15 A Random Selection of Files and Folders

- To select random objects, as above, hold the **Ctrl** key down and left-click them, one by one.

- To select all the items in a window just use the **Ctrl+A** keyboard shortcut.

To cancel a selection, click in an empty area of the window.

Copying Files and Folders – When you *copy* a file or folder to somewhere else, the original version of the folder or file is not altered or removed, but when you *move* a folder or file to a new location, the original is actually deleted.

To copy selected items into another folder, right-click them and choose the **Copy** option from the shortcut menu. They are then copied to the Windows **Clipboard** which is a temporary storage area in memory where text, graphics and files are stored with the Windows **Cut** and **Copy** commands.

All you need to do now is navigate to the destination folder, right-click in it and select the **Paste** option from the context, or shortcut menu that opens.

Moving Files and Folders – To move selected items into a target folder, choose the **Cut** option from the shortcut menu. This removes them from their current place and copies them to the Windows **Clipboard** so that you can **Paste** them into the target folder.

Using Drag and Drop – If you are happy using the mouse, you can drag selected objects in one folder or between two open folders, with the **Ctrl** key depressed, to copy them.

If you don't use the **Ctrl** key you will move them. You need to be careful with this method though, as it is easy to drop your precious files and folders in the wrong location. You then have to spend 'hours' looking for them!

Creating Desktop Shortcuts – With Windows you can put a shortcut to any program file or document on your Desktop or in a folder. Shortcuts are quick ways to get to the items you use often; they save you having to dig into menus to access them.

The easiest way to do this is to find the program in the **Start**, **All Programs** list and drag it to the Desktop with the right mouse button depressed. When the mouse button is released, select the **Create shortcuts here** option from the menu that opens. This places the new shortcut on the Desktop and you can drag it to the location on your screen that you want. Fig. 4.16 below shows the sequence graphically for creating a shortcut to the WordPad program.

Double-clicking a shortcut icon on the Desktop is much easier than digging deep into the menus to open a program.

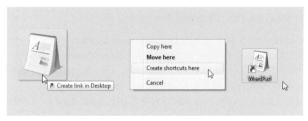

Fig. 4.16 Creating a Shortcut on the Desktop

Deleting Files or Folders – To delete or remove files or folders, first select them in an Explorer window, and then either select the **Organize**, **Delete** option, right-click them and select **Delete**, or press the **Del** key on the keyboard. All of these methods open a message box giving you the chance to abort the operation by selecting **No**.

Deleting a single folder or file displays a dialogue box similar to that shown in Fig 4.17.

Fig. 4.17 The Delete Folder Warning Box

In any of these cases, to carry on with the deletion, select the **Yes** option.

Perhaps now is the time to do some housekeeping and delete any duplicate or unwanted image files. Take care though and make sure you really don't want them! Do carry out this suggestion as we need to demonstrate what happens to deleted items next.

The Recycle Bin

As you can see from the **Delete Folder** message box above, by default all files or folders deleted from a hard disc, are actually placed in a holding folder named the **Recycle Bin**.

If you open the **Recycle Bin**, by double-clicking its Desktop icon, shown here, you will see that it is just a special folder. It lists all the files, folders, icons and shortcuts that have been deleted from fixed drives since it was last emptied, as shown in Fig. 4.18 on the next page.

Fig. 4.18 Emptying the Recycle Bin

Windows 7 keeps a record of the original locations of the deleted files and folders, so that it can restore them if necessary. To restore all the items in the **Recycle Bin**, click the **Restore all items** button. To finally delete its contents click the **Empty the Recycle Bin** option pointed to above. Beware though, you won't be able to get the data back again.

To restore specific files or folders, first select them, then click the **Restore selected items** button. To delete an item, select it and press the **Delete** keyboard key.

Every now and then you should open the **Recycle Bin** and delete unwanted files or folders to free up hard disc space.

Sorting and Filtering

As long as you are in **Details** view, you can control what files are displayed in an Explorer window (filtering) and in what order (sorting). You do this by clicking the headings above the file list.

Just clicking a header will sort the displayed files based on the header. The **Name** header sorts alphabetically, **Size** sorts by file size, etc. Clicking the header again reverses the sort order. In Fig. 4.19 we sorted the files alphabetically by clicking the **Name** header, as shown. Folders are sorted first in the listing, followed by files.

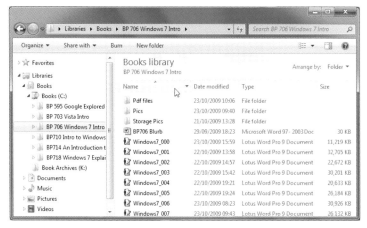

Fig. 4.19 A Folder Sorted by Name

You filter your files when you only want ones with a particular property to be displayed. You do this by clicking the arrow to the right of the heading that you want to filter by. The drop-down menu that opens, depends on the heading clicked. In Fig. 4.20 for instance, you can select to only show files that were last modified in a certain date range, by clicking the arrow to the right of the **Date modified** heading, and selecting the date range in the 'calendar box', or by ticking the boxes next to the types you want.

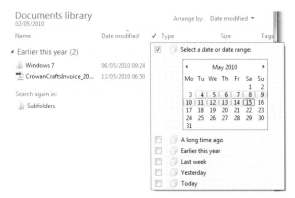

Fig. 4.20 Date Filtering a Folder

Copying to a CD or DVD

To copy files or folders to a CD or DVD, you will need a disc recorder fitted to your PC and a supply of suitable discs.

By default, Windows 7 uses the **Live File System** format for burning CDs and DVDs. With this format you can copy selected files immediately and as often as you want straight to the disc in the recorder drive, just like a USB flash drive or floppy disc. BUT, the discs produced are only compatible with Windows XP, Vista, and Windows 7.

To start the process, locate and select the files or folders you want to copy to disc. Make sure that they do not exceed 650 MB for a standard CD or 4.7 GB for a standard DVD. Click the **Burn** button 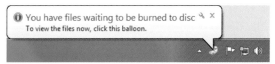 on the Explorer window toolbar, as shown earlier in Fig. 4.15. A balloon message may open on the Taskbar as shown in Fig. 4.21, or you may just be asked to **Insert a disc**.

ⓘ You have files waiting to be burned to disc ✎ ✕
To view the files now, click this balloon.

Fig. 4.21 A CD Burn Notification Message

If you insert a blank recordable or rewritable CD or DVD in the recorder when asked, the format procedure will start. Type a title in the **Burn a Disc** box that opens (Fig. 4.22).

When you click the **Next** button, Windows will format the disc after first checking with you. This took a few minutes for us with a new CD-RW disc. A DVD would take longer. But it only needs doing once.

Fig. 4.22 Preparing a Blank Disc

Fig. 4.23 Burning Selected Files to a CD

When the formatting is complete a new Explorer window opens onto the CD drive. In the future you can simply drag selected files into this window, or click the **Burn** button on the toolbar. The burning process is then started and the selected files are copied to the disc, as shown in Fig. 4.23.

You can leave the disc in the drive while you are working and copy more files to it, or delete files from it, whenever you want. This method is useful for making manual backup type copies of your data.

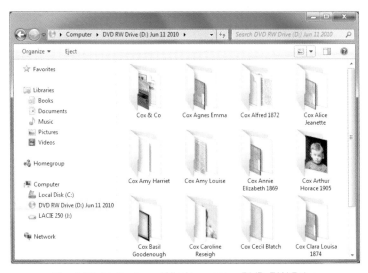

Fig. 4.24 An Explorer Window onto a DVD-RW Drive

Burning a DVD from an ISO File

If you download Windows 7 or other program updates from the Internet they will probably come as an ISO file or disc image. This is a single file which is a copy of an entire data CD or DVD. When you burn a CD or DVD from such an ISO file, the new disc you create will have the same folders, files, and properties as the original disc.

Windows 7 handles this procedure almost automatically. You just insert a recordable disc into your disc burner, locate the ISO file in an Explorer window and double-click it.

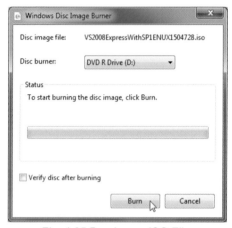

Fig. 4.25 Burning an ISO File

It's a good idea to verify that the disc image is burned correctly by selecting the **Verify disc after burning** check box. Finally clicking the **Burn** button will start the procedure.

Context Menus

In Windows 7 you can right-click on most screen objects to open a context menu of options that you can carry out. In Fig. 4.26 below we have right-clicked on an image in an Explorer window.

Sending Files and Folders

A very useful feature in Windows is the ability to quickly send files and folders to specific destinations.

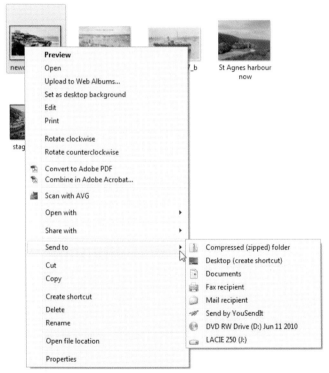

Fig. 4.26 A Right-click Context Menu with Send to Options

Selecting the **Send to** option opens the list of available destinations. In your case these are bound to be different.

As an example, selecting the **DVD RW Drive (D:)** option will copy any selected folders and files to a removable disc in the (D:) drive, provided there is enough room.

Compressing Files and Folders

Another useful feature on the **Send to** sub menu of Fig. 4.26 is the Compressed (zipped) folder option. Compressing files and folders allows you to greatly increase the storage capacity of your hard disc and also increases the amount of data you can copy to a single CD.

As an example we selected all the files and folders for an earlier book in an Explorer window, which together were 312 MB in size. We right-clicked the selection, pointed to the **Send to** option on the drop-down menu, and clicked the **Compressed (zipped) folder** option.

After about 4 minutes a **.zip** folder was created and given the same name as one of the selected folders. Windows 7 automatically gives the folder that contains the zipped files the same name as one of the selected files. You can of course rename it, but remember to keep the **.zip** extension.

You can add other files and folders into the compressed folder by dragging them into it. Selected files are then compressed one at time before they are moved into the folder.

To find out the size of the folder's contents before and after compression, right-click it and select **Properties** from the drop-down menu. In our case the size of the folder was 312 MB before compression, and 171 MB after compression; a large enough compression ratio and worth exploiting.

You can open files and programs in a compressed folder by double-clicking them. To extract a file or folder from a compressed folder, simply drag it to its new location. To extract all files and folders within a compressed folder, right-click the folder and select **Extract All**. You can specify where you want these files and folders to be extracted to.

Useful Things to Do

Before we leave this section we will just include a few quick operations that should make using Windows 7 a little easier.

Adding Favorite Links

Customising the **Favorites** links in the Navigation Pane on the left side of Explorer windows can be a tremendous time saver. You can drag and drop your favourite and most commonly accessed folders and drives, either on your own PC or on a local network.

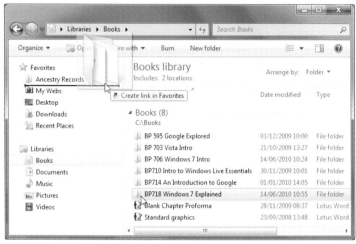

Fig. 4.27 Adding a Link to the Favorites List

In Fig. 4.27 above we are in the process of creating a link in the **Favorites** section of the Navigation Pane to the folder on our PC containing all the files for this book.

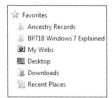

It is just a case of clicking the folder, dragging it into the **Favorites** section, and releasing the mouse button when the black line is where you want to place the link. In the future, clicking this link will open the folder, wherever you are.

Using the Details Pane

The Details Pane along the bottom of Explorer windows is interactive; you can use it to add and update information about a file, such as its Title, Tags or a Rating.

Fig. 4.28 Opening the Details Pane

As shown above, to open the Details Pane just press the **Organize** button and select **Layout**, **Details pane**.

If you want more details about the files, you can right-click in the Details Pane when no file is selected and change its size. The bigger it is, the more information is displayed, as shown later for pictures on page 63.

Pinning Programs to the Taskbar

To pin your most used programs to the Taskbar and always have them instantly available, either right-click on their entry in the **Start** Menu and select **Pin to Taskbar** from the context menu, or if they are actually running, right-click on their icon in the Taskbar and select **Pin to Taskbar**.

5

Working with Pictures

Photographs

As we have seen, in Windows 7 the **Pictures Library** points to the **My Pictures** folder provided for storing all of your digital pictures. It is the default location for saving pictures and importing them from your digital camera or scanner. We put most of our images in sub-folders of the **My Pictures** folder, as it makes it easier to keep track of them. Fig. 5.1 shows a folder of our photos taken on a recent trip.

Fig. 5.1 A Folder of Digital Photographs

Picture Windows

You have probably noticed by now that a window's toolbar buttons change depending on what you are doing. Fig. 5.1 shows a typical **Pictures** window toolbar with a file selected. If nothing is selected, the buttons on the bar change to those shown in Fig. 5.2 below.

Fig. 5.2 A Pictures Folder Toolbar

Preview Pane

To see a larger preview of a picture thumbnail you can click the **Show the preview pane** button ⬚ on the toolbar, or use the new **Alt+P** keyboard shortcut, and then click the thumbnail, as we have done below.

Fig. 5.3 The Preview Pane

The Windows Photo Viewer

By default, double-clicking a picture thumbnail in an Explorer folder, or clicking the **Preview** toolbar button , opens the **Windows Photo Viewer**, as shown in Fig. 5.4.

Fig. 5.4 'Cooling Off' in the Windows Photo Viewer

The Toolbar at the top of this window offers similar options to those of the original Explorer window. You can use the controls at the bottom to navigate through the current folder, view the pictures in your folder as a slide show, zoom in or out, rotate the image, and delete it from your hard disc.

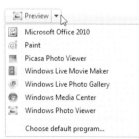

Fig. 5.5 Program Options

Clicking the down-arrow next to the **Preview** button of an Explorer window, opens a list of other programs available on your PC for viewing or possibly editing photo files.

Printing Photos

Selecting pictures in a window and clicking the **Print** button ⬚Print⬚, displays the Print Pictures window shown below.

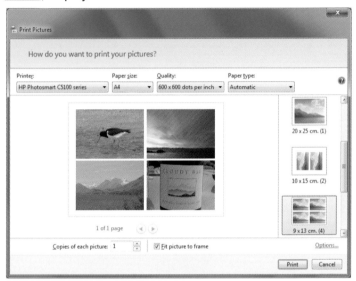

Fig. 5.6 Printing Photos from an Explorer Window

From here you can select the **Printer** to be used, **Paper size**, **Quality** of print, **Paper Type** and a variety of layouts for your pictures. All you have to do then is click the **Print** button.

Slide Show

Clicking the **Slide show** button ⬚Slide show⬚ starts a full-screen slide show of any selected photos or videos in the current folder. You close, or control the show, from its right-click menu shown in Fig. 5.7.

Fig. 5.7 Slide Show Controls

Tagging Pictures

With digital cameras it is very easy and cheap to take large numbers of photographs and store them on your computer, which usually means that finding a particular picture is difficult. You can make it easier though if you add descriptive labels, or tags, to your pictures.

You do this in the Details Pane (page 58) opened by clicking the **Organize** button and selecting **Layout**, **Details pane**. Once it is open you can right-click in the Details Pane when no file is selected and change its size from the drop-down menu shown in Fig. 5.8.

Fig. 5.8 Changing the Size of the Details Pane

You can add tags in all three sizes, but the bigger the pane, the more information is displayed, as shown below.

Fig. 5.9 A Typical Details Pane in Small, Medium and Large Sizes

To add tags, click to select the picture that you want to tag, or for multiple pictures, hold down the **Ctrl** key, and then click all the pictures in a folder that you want to give the same tag.

In the Details Pane at the bottom of the window, in the Text box next to **Tags:**, click **Add a tag**, and overtype with a suitable tag name (maybe to identify the location, a person, or the event), and then click the **Save** button that opens. You can add multiple tags to a picture by typing a semicolon (;) between each tag.

In the Details Pane, you can also add a title, a rating (from one to five) or change the date the picture was taken. The Tags information is saved with the EXIF (Exchangeable Image File) data 'attached' to the photograph file. Most digital cameras save **.jpg** files including EXIF information of the camera settings and other information recorded by the camera. To see this information, right-click a thumbnail in a Pictures folder, select the **Properties** option and open the Details tab as shown in Fig. 5.10 for one of our photos.

Fig. 5.10 Some of the EXIF Details of a Photograph

If you view the properties of your photographs in an external program, such as Google Picasa, only the tag information you added will be included in the photos 'meta data'. Shame!

Searching the Pictures Library

Once you have added tags to your photos it is very easy to search for photos with specific tags.

To find a photo by its tags (or by its file name) just type the tag or name of the file into the **Search** box at the top right of the pictures window. Sometimes just typing the first few letters is enough.

Fig. 5.11 Results of a Photo Tag Search

In Fig. 5.11 above we searched our NZ Trip folder for the tag 'kea'. The photo was found almost instantly. We could also have searched the Pictures Library in the same way, when all our photos would have been included in the search.

Fig. 5.12 Using a Tags
Filter Search

If you don't want to type the tag text in a tag search, click the **Search** box, and click **Tags** as shown in Fig. 5.12. This opens a menu listing of all the tags in the current folder or Library. Clicking a tag in this list will show all the pictures using it.

To return to the Pictures library after searching, click the **Back** button .

Getting Photos from a Camera

There are many ways to import pictures from your digital camera to your computer. Some involve using third party software or programs included with the camera. With Windows 7 though you can do it very simply.

Once you have taken a batch of photos, connect the

camera to your computer with the USB cable (that almost certainly came with the camera) and switch the camera on.

An AutoPlay box should open similar to ours in Fig. 5.13. In our case Windows 7 hasn't recognised the camera as such, but has designated it as Removable Disk (K:). Yours will probably be different. Click the **Import pictures and videos** using Windows option.

Fig. 5.13 The Autoplay Box

To give all the imported photos a common tag type a tag name in the **Tag these pictures (optional)** box that opens next.

Fig. 5.14 Adding a Common Tag to Imported Photos

In our case in Fig. 5.14 all the photos to be imported were taken in and around Falmouth Harbour, so we have used that as a common tag. Then click the **Import** button.

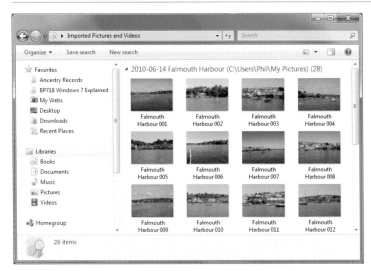

Fig. 5.15 Imported Photos in a New Windows Folder

A new folder is opened for the imported photos as shown in Fig. 5.15 above.

By default, the new folder is placed in the Pictures Library and given a name made up from the date the pictures were imported and the tag name, **2010-06-14 Falmouth Harbour** in our case. Each imported photograph is given a name also based on the tag.

If you are happy with this, fine. If not you can spend a while renaming files and the folder.

In this case in the future you would probably be happier either:

- clicking the **Import settings** option shown in Fig. 5.14 to customise the importing procedure yourself, or

- selecting the **Open folder to view files** using Windows explorer option in the Autoplay box of Fig. 5.13. You can then manually copy and paste the photos from your camera to whatever new folder you want on the computer.

Scanning Photos

To import the images from paper photographs or slides into your computer you have to use a scanner. These are fairly cheap these days, in fact many printers include the ability to scan as well. To handle slides effectively though you need a special slide and negative scanner, but be warned these are not cheap!

Windows Fax and Scan

There are many ways to control a scanner using third party software but Windows 7 comes with its own program called Windows Fax and Scan. This was included in the high-end versions of Windows Vista, but comes with all the versions of Windows 7. It looks a bit dated, but still works quite well.

With your scanner properly installed and turned on you can open this program by clicking the **Start** button 🔵, clicking **All Programs**, and selecting 🖼 Windows Fax and Scan from the list that opens.

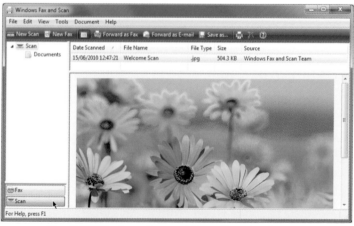

Fig. 5.16 Windows Fax and Scan Opening Screen

To get started, place your photo on the scanner tray and click the **Scan** button at the bottom of the left pane (pointed to in Fig. 5.16 above). Then click the 🖼 New Scan toolbar button .

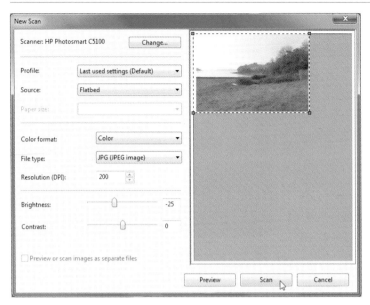

Fig. 5.17 Scanning a Photograph

The New Scan dialogue box opens with the default settings for scanning a photo as shown in Fig. 5.17. Clicking the **Preview** button shows you how the photo will appear when scanned. You control the actual area scanned by dragging the handles of the cropping tool as shown above. If necessary you can change the scan settings, and then click the **Scan** button.

Scanned photos are automatically saved in the Scanned Documents folder in the Documents Library and given the names, Image, Image1, etc... To change the file name, right-click the default name in the Scan view, and select **Rename** from the drop-down menu.

Fig. 5.18 on the next page shows this procedure. Here we have added a folder called Photos by right-clicking the Scan folder button ⬛ Scan in the left pane, and clicking the **New Folder** option. For some reason, the new folder does not show in the Scan view until you collapse and then expand the list of folders.

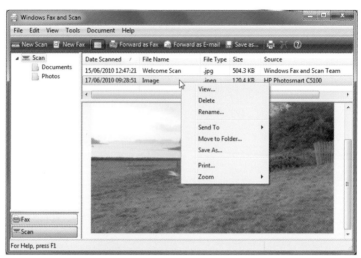

Fig. 5.18 Renaming and Moving a Scanned Image

Once you have renamed your scanned image, you can right-click it again, select **Move to Folder** and move it to the Photos folder; or anywhere else if you prefer.

The Windows Fax and Scan program is not particularly intuitive for photos, but it is easy enough to work with. It was really designed for scanning documents.

Device Stage

In Windows 7, working with printers, scanners, cameras, mobile phones, and other devices can be easier than with older versions of Windows, thanks to a new feature, Device Stage. This is a visual interface that provides a way for you to interact with devices that support it. Manufacturers can customise Device Stage for their products to show the current status of a device and give visual menu options so that you can easily control its functions.

For compatible cameras for instance, Device Stage will open instead of AutoPlay when you connect them to your computer and turn them on. Then to import pictures, you click the **Import** link in Device Stage.

When Device Stage compatible printers and scanners are plugged into a computer running Windows 7 (usually with a USB cable) Windows 7 automatically downloads and installs any required drivers and places an icon to control the device in the **Devices and Printers** folder.

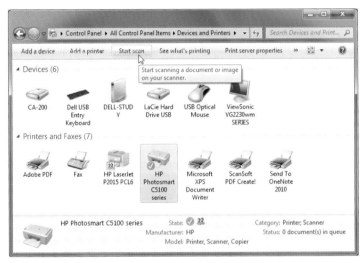

Fig. 5.19 Our Devices and Printers Folder

To open this folder you simply click the Start button 🌐, and click the Devices and Printers option [Devices and Printers] in the menu on the right.

Clicking a device icon in this folder opens a contextual toolbar at the top, as in Fig. 5.19 above. Here our HP printer, scanner, copier was selected and a **Start scan** button was available. Clicking this starts the scanning operation.

When you double-click a **Device Stage** icon, the device window is opened and an icon is placed on the Taskbar. The window is designed by the company that made the device, HP in our case as shown in Fig. 5.20 on the next page. It contains status information and menu options to control the printing and scanning operations.

Your device will probably be different but the principles will be the same.

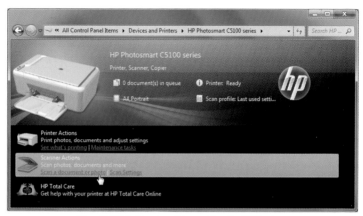

Fig. 5.20 A Device Stage Control Window

Fig. 5.21 Jump List

We can click the **Scan a document or photo** link pointed to above to start scanning.

We don't spend a lot of time on this page, though, as most of the options are more easily available by right-clicking the device icon on the Windows Taskbar. This opens a Jump List menu as shown in Fig. 5.21. The window still has to be open of course, but we can minimise it to 'hide' it.

The advantage of this method of scanning is that once a scan has taken place it opens the **Import Pictures and Videos** box we showed earlier in Fig. 5.14. The procedure for tagging, naming and saving your scanned images is then the same as described on pages 66 and 67.

Windows Live Photo Gallery

With Windows 7 Microsoft have left out many of the components that were included with earlier versions of the operating system. It does not, for instance, come packaged with a program for handling and editing photographs.

This is not a problem though, as Microsoft has made **Windows Live Essentials** available as a free optional download. This includes a number of new versions of applications designed to work with Windows 7, including **Windows Live Photo Gallery**. Please see page 116 for details of how to carry out the download.

Fig. 5.22 Windows Live Photo Gallery

With the **Windows Live Photo Gallery** you can view, edit and sort your photos and display them in different ways; by date, using star ratings, or using descriptive tags.

Once your photos have been fixed and organised, you can save a folder of photos to a blank CD or DVD, or click a button to make a slide show with **Windows Live Movie Maker**.

Windows Live Photo Gallery also makes it very easy to import photos from cameras and scanners. Perhaps more exploration is required here! You could even look for our book BP710 - *An Introduction to Windows Live Essentials* by N. Kantaris and P.R.M. Oliver, ISBN 978 0 85934 710 5, priced at £6.99.

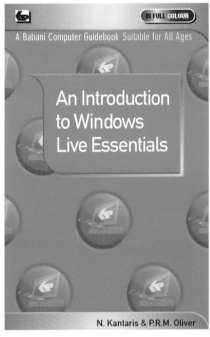

Fig. 5.23 Front Cover of *An Introduction to Windows Live Essentials*

6

Handling Music and Media

Windows 7 has been designed for handling all your digital media content, such as digital music, videos, photos, recorded TV shows and streamed Internet media.

  We have already looked at photos, but two other libraries are provided for storing your Music and Videos files, as shown here. By default, media files will be saved to these libraries automatically by the media programs described here.

Windows Media Player

 Windows Media Player is the main media 'workhorse' in Windows 7. It has been around for a few years now and for us Version 12 was installed with Windows 7. It provides a good-looking, intuitive and easy-to-use interface for you to play the digital media files stored on your computer, or on CDs or DVDs, or other external storage devices. You can organise your digital media collection, rip music from your CDs to the computer and burn CDs of your favourite music, so you can play them on your home system or in your car.

It also lets you sync (synchronise) digital media files to a large range of portable media devices (but not Apple iPods and iPads unfortunately), and encourages you to shop for digital media content online.

In other words, with Media Player you can play your audio and video material, view it, organise it, or sync it.

Starting Media Player

By default, clicking the **Windows Media Player** button  which is placed on the Taskbar when Windows 7 is first installed will open the program.

Alternatively, to start Media Player, click the **Start** button 🌐 on the left of the Taskbar, to open the **Start** menu. Then just start typing 'media player' into the **Search programs and files** box shown here. Before you have entered the first few letters the Windows Media Player option will appear at the top of the results list. You click this to open the Player.

Media Player gives many views onto your media, but it might when started look something like ours in Fig. 6.1 below.

Fig. 6.1 A Player Library View of Some of our Music

This view shows an alphabetic listing of the Artists in our music collection using the Tiles view option which gives some details of the CDs and tracks for each artist.

Monitoring Folders

When you start the Player for the first time you are asked to choose some settings, then it automatically searches the default folders included in the Music, Pictures, Videos, (and possibly Recorded TV) libraries on your computer. If you ever change the files from these media libraries, the Player will automatically update its available media files the next time it starts up. To build your media library, you can also include folders in the libraries from other locations on your computer or external devices, such as portable hard drives, or storage devices.

Player View Modes

Media Player lets you toggle between two main view modes. The Player Library shown in Fig. 6.1, which gives you control of all the Player's features, and a Now Playing mode (Fig. 6.2), which gives a simplified view ideal for playback.

Fig. 6.2 Now Playing Mode

To move between these modes click the **Switch to Now Playing** button, or from the Player, the **Switch to Library** button in the upper-right corner.

There are two other view modes available.

Skin mode – gives customised views of the Player. Use the **Ctrl+2** keys together to change the Player to Skin mode. Two skins are included. You can change between these or download other skins with the **View**, **Skin chooser** menu command. We will leave it to you to explore this mode further.

Fig. 6.3
The Revert Skin Mode

Full-screen mode – makes pictures, videos, and DVDs fill the entire screen when you play them. You just click the **View full screen** button 🖼 in the lower-right corner of the Player, or press the **Alt+Enter** keys.

Player Library Mode

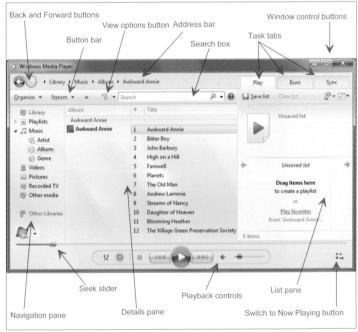

Fig. 6.4 Parts of the Player Library Window

When you click an item, such as **Music**, in the Navigation pane it lists your media content in the Details Pane. As we show in Fig. 6.1 clicking on **Artist** will list your music files by artist and double-clicking on a CD icon lists the tracks on that CD. Double-clicking on a track name will start it playing in the Media Player.

As you move through your library this way, look at the Address bar along the top. As with other Explorer windows (see page 42) you can also click on the 'breadcrumbs' on the bar to access all the levels of your library.

Fig. 6.5 Navigating a Library with the Address Bar

You can also use the Back and Forward buttons to step through your previous route.

There are three different viewing options in the Details Pane, chosen from a drop-down menu by clicking the arrow next to the **View options** button, or by just clicking the button itself until you get the view you want.

Icon view – Windows Media Player 12 uses the album art (downloaded cover pictures) of your CDs to create icons. How much information is displayed below the album cover 'stack' depends on which level of the library you are viewing. In our example here, we were at the Artist level, so it shows the artist name below the icon. At the Album level the album name is displayed as well.

Tile View – With this view you get the album artwork with more information displayed to the right. In the Album level, you get the artist name, album name, genre and year. In the Artist view (shown

here), you also get the number of albums, songs and the total playing length. If your albums are star rated, this information is shown as well.

Details View – This view shows the category columns for an artist or album, such as Album, Album artist, Genre, Release year, Count (number of tracks), Length and Rating.

This view is customisable and useful for sorting and searching your library. To sort your songs according to a particular category or column just click the column header to sort the items in ascending order. Clicking it again will reverse the sort order.

Searching a Library

When you want to find a specific artist, album title or song name, you can simply type a search string in the **Search** box as we have done in Fig. 6.6. We typed **dylan** which immediately presented details of the three Bob Dylan albums we have saved.

Fig. 6.6 Searching for Specific Music

Double-clicking on an album in the list opens the album so that you can see all the track details as in Fig. 6.7.

Fig. 6.7 An Album's Contents Shown as an Expanded Tile

To play a song either double-click it in the list, or highlight it and press the **Play** button in the Playback controls at the bottom of the window and pointed to above.

Previewing Music

Fig. 6.8 The Preview Button

If you hover your mouse over a song in a listing, a box pops up with a **Preview** button, as shown in Fig. 6.8. Clicking this button starts the song playing in Preview Mode. You can skip 15 seconds into the song by clicking **Skip**. When you move your mouse away from the Preview box the track will automatically stop playing. This is a useful feature if you just want to hear what the song sounds like.

Playback Controls

The Playback Controls are always visible at the bottom of the Player Library.

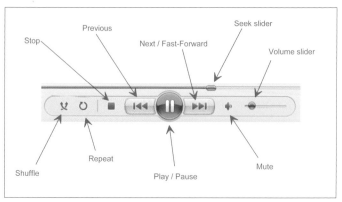

Fig. 6.9 The Player Library Playback Controls

The functions of these controls are similar to a normal CD player, from left to right they are:

Shuffle	Tracks in the selected album, playlist or category are played in a random order. Toggle to turn off the feature.
Repeat	Repeats the selected playlist, album or category. To play one song continuously, play it from a search query or create a playlist containing that one song only. Toggle to turn off the feature.
Stop	Ceases playback and resets the Play Position to the beginning of the track or song.
Previous	Returns to the previous song in the playlist or category selected. In Shuffle Mode, this button plays the song that was played previously, regardless of its position in the playlist.

Play/Pause 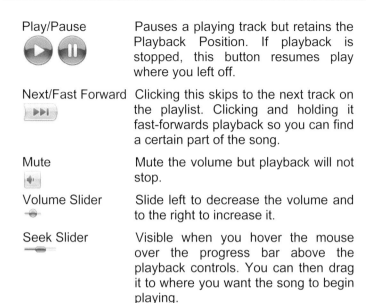	Pauses a playing track but retains the Playback Position. If playback is stopped, this button resumes play where you left off.
Next/Fast Forward	Clicking this skips to the next track on the playlist. Clicking and holding it fast-forwards playback so you can find a certain part of the song.
Mute	Mute the volume but playback will not stop.
Volume Slider	Slide left to decrease the volume and to the right to increase it.
Seek Slider	Visible when you hover the mouse over the progress bar above the playback controls. You can then drag it to where you want the song to begin playing.

The area to the left of the Playback Controls gives you information on what is actually being played. Fig. 6.10 shows the artist and album artwork.

Fig. 6.10 Track Information

If you click the album cover it will disappear. Clicking again switches to an equaliser display, and clicking again switches back to the artwork. The text to the right phases through the following information for the music currently playing; album title, the track playing, the artist and the composer (Johny Cash the artist in Fig. 6.10).

Immediately to the left of the Playback Controls is a counter which shows how much of the current track has been played. If you double-click on the counter it changes to show the length of the current track as well 01:56 / 03:42 .

When you drag the **Seek** slider ——— your location in the current track is shown on this counter.

Playing from the Taskbar

With Windows 7 you can play songs and to some extent control Media Player 12 right from the Taskbar.

Fig. 6.11 Using the Media Player Taskbar Button

With a music track or video playing, hover the mouse over the **Media Player** icon in the Taskbar as shown in Fig. 6.11 above. Playback Controls appear and the artist and name of the item playing are shown in a 'popup' above. Between is a live preview thumbnail which shows whatever else is happening in the Player at the time, such as album art, a playing video, visualisations, etc.

You can click the **Previous** ⏮, **Play** ▶, **Pause** ⏸, or **Next** ⏭ controls just like you would in the Player Library.

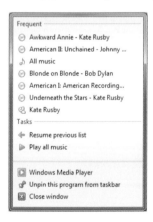

If you right-click the Media Player icon in the Taskbar a jump-list menu appears which gives you rapid access to your most frequently played media, as well as other tasks.

Fig. 6.12 A Jump List Menu

Now Playing Mode

In Now Playing mode, accessed from the Player Library by clicking the **Switch to Now Playing** button, you can see what music is currently playing, or view DVDs and videos in a small and compact window. This fits easily on your screen area amongst your other working windows.

Fig. 6.13 Playing a CD in Now Playing Mode

When you move the mouse pointer over this window the playback controls appear as shown in Fig. 6.13. But if the window is too small not all of them may show.

If you right-click the Now Playing window an extensive context menu of available actions opens, as shown here in Fig. 6.14.

Clicking the **Show list** option opens the list of what is currently playing, as shown in Fig. 6.15 on the next page.

Fig. 6.14 The Now Playing Menu

Fig. 6.15 Now Playing Mode with Playing List Showing

This is our preferred set-up when using Media Player to play the music on our computers.

Playing Audio CDs

So far we have dealt with playing the music already in your Library collection. To play an audio CD, just insert the disc into the DVD or CD drive of your computer and by default Windows Media Player will open with the CD playing and with an icon in the Navigation Pane something like ⊙ MCMXC A.D. (D:).

If an **AutoPlay** box opens, like the one here, select the **Play audio CD using Windows Media Player** option to start the procedure.

Fig. 6.16 The AutoPlay Menu

Ripping from Audio CDs

The tracks and songs on an inserted CD will not show in your Library unless you 'rip' them from the CD. This is not as destructive as it sounds. It simply means copying tracks from the CD to the library on your computer hard disc, so that you can listen to them whenever you want to.

To rip tracks from an audio CD, put the CD into the drive, and after a few seconds your computer should recognise it and download the disc's details from the Internet. If necessary switch to Player Library view and click on the CD icon in the Navigation Pane.

Fig. 6.17 Getting Ready to Rip a CD

The Details pane should display the album art and all the album tracks named and selected to be copied to your library, as shown in Fig. 6.17 above. If the Player does not recognise the CD automatically it will show as an **Unknown album**. It is usually easy to correct this by right-clicking the default album artwork graphic shown here and selecting the **Find album info** option. Then type the artist's name and the album title in the **Search** box, click the **Search** button and hopefully select the correct album from the list offered, as in Fig. 6.18.

Then click the **Next** button, check that the track information is correct and finally select **Finish** to accept the info shown.

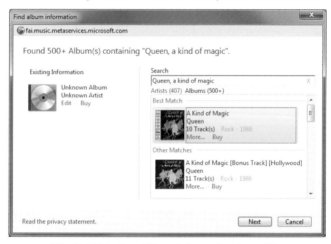

Fig. 6.18 Finding Album Information for a CD

By default, Windows Media Player 12 rips to **.wma** format with CD quality encoding. This is good enough for us but if you want to change these settings click **Rip settings** on the Button bar and choose **More options**.

If there are any tracks that you don't want to rip, clear the check box next to them (Fig. 6.17). When you are ready, click the **Rip CD** button on the Button bar to start the process.

By default the selected tracks are copied to the Music library on your PC with folders added and labelled with the name of the artist or group.

While the ripping operation is in progress you can see exactly what is going on by looking at the Rip status column. You can listen to the CD while you are ripping it, so you needn't get too bored.

To cancel the operation at any time just click the **Stop rip** button . Once you have done one CD you will find it very easy to rip your whole collection.

Using Playlists

A playlist is a saved list of media items (such as songs) which appears in your Library on the left side in the Navigation

Fig. 6.19 List Pane

Pane. Creating, saving and editing Media Player playlists of your favourite tracks is very easy.

You do it in the List Pane shown in Fig. 6.19 which is opened when you click the Play tab.

If there are items in the list, click **Clear list** to remove them. To name a new playlist click the **Unsaved list** text item pointed to in Fig. 6.19, type a name and click the **Save list** button. You should do this whenever you make changes.

To add songs to the playlist find them in your Player Library and just drag and drop them into the new list. Or you can right-click the song, choose **Add to** and select the list to add it to, even if that list is not open in the List Pane.

Once you have songs in your playlist, you can move them about and edit them by right-clicking and choosing **Remove from list** or **Move up** or **Move down**. You can also reorder them by dragging and dropping them within the list. For more options, click the **List options** button in the top-right corner of the List Pane.

Here, you can sort your list according to attributes such as artist name, title, album and length. This is similar to sorting songs by columns. Clicking **Shuffle list** rearranges the items in your playlist in a random order.

Once you have created and saved a list it shows in the **Playlists** item in the Navigation Pane, as shown here.

Burning CDs and DVDs

With Media Player 12 you can burn, or create, CD-R and CD-RW type CDs and DVDs, as long as you have a suitable recorder on your PC. To begin, insert a blank CD or DVD into your disc drive. If the AutoPlay window pops up, choose **Burn an audio CD** using Windows Media Player. If not simply open Windows Media Player 12 as usual.

You do it in the Burn List Pane shown in Fig. 6.20. This should appear automatically, but if it doesn't just click the Burn tab.

If there are items in the list, click **Clear list** to remove them. To name the new disc click the **Burn list** text item pointed to in Fig. 6.20, and type a name for it. This will show up on CD players that support CD text.

As with a playlist, to add songs to the Burn list find them in your Player Library and drag and drop them into the new list.

Fig. 6.20 The Burn List Pane

If necessary you next choose the Disc Type you want to burn. There are three different types of discs you can burn:

Audio CD – These hold about 80 minutes of music, are readable by computers and are playable in any CD player. This type was automatically selected in our example above.

Data CD – These hold about 700 MB of data, are readable by computers and CD players that support playback of digital audio files. They are not playable on standard CD players.

Data DVD – These hold about 4 GB of data and are readable by DVD players that support playback of digital audio files. They are primarily intended to be readable by computers.

To choose the type of disc to burn, click the **Burn options** button ⌨▾ in the top right corner and choose from the drop-down menu. You can also adjust other options by clicking **More burn options** which opens the Media Player **Options** box shown below.

Fig. 6.21 Windows Media Player 12 Options Box

When you are happy with your settings, click **Apply** and **OK**, followed by the **Start burn** button 🞛 Start burn.

When the burn begins, the status is shown in a green bar at the top of the Burn List. Clicking the blue text link below it lets you see the status of each individual track.

Quite a straightforward operation. We use this method to create audio CDs to use in our car on those long boring trips, to drown out the kids pleas of "Are we there yet?"

Fig. 6.22 Burn Status

Playing Videos and DVDs

Playing videos from Media Player is similar to playing audio files, you simply click **Videos** in the Navigation Pane and double-click a file to play it.

Fig. 6.23 Some Videos in our Video Library

Fig. 6.24 A Video in a Now Playing Window

A video plays in the **Now Playing** mode in a window that is optimised for its properties as shown in Fig. 6.24 on the facing page. All the controls appear when you move the mouse pointer over the window, as well as the **View full screen** and **Switch to Library** buttons.

Playing DVDs

Windows Media Player 12 plays DVD videos. To watch a DVD on your PC, insert the disc into your DVD drive and by

default it will start playing straight away.

If the AutoPlay window opens instead, choose the **Play DVD movie** using Windows Media Player option as shown here in Fig. 6.25.

You can make this the default setting by checking the **Always do this for DVD movies** check box, as we have done.

Fig. 6.25 The AutoPlay Window

Fig. 6.26 Start Menu of a DVD with Playing Controls

The DVD will start playing in a **Now Playing** window, as shown in Fig. 6.26, or maybe full screen. As with video playback, all the controls appear when you move the mouse pointer over the window, but a DVD button DVD is added. Clicking this brings you back to the DVD title menu (Fig. 6.26). Clicking the little arrow to the right brings up other options to control the playback. We will leave it to you to explore these.

If you click the **Switch to Library** button you can view all of the DVD chapters and titles and start playback from any location.

The Sync Function

You can use the Media Player to sync (or copy) music, videos, and pictures to a wide range of portable devices, including portable media players, storage cards, and some mobile phones. To do this, you connect a supported device to your computer and the Player will select the sync method (automatic or manual) that is best for the device and open the Sync tab. Then, you can sync the files and playlists in your Player Library to your device, by just dragging them to the Sync list as described in earlier sections.

Unfortunately Microsoft and Apple don't get on too well and you can't sync with Apple devices like the iPod and iPad. So if you have one of these you will have to stay with iTunes.

Help and Support

We have run out of space for the Media Player so will leave it up to you to explore its other features such as; streaming your music over the Internet or your own network, sorting your photographs, and using the **Media Guide** button Media Guide to visit WindowsMedia.com and to listen to Internet radio.

At any time you can press the **F1** key from the Media Player to get detailed **Help and Support**.

Windows Media Center

We don't think many people use Windows Media Center and that is a shame. It was designed to serve as a home-entertainment hub for the living-room TV and is included in Windows 7 (except the Starter version). If you have a TV tuner for your computer you can watch, pause, and record live TV, if not, there is still Internet TV which offers online shows and movies. But it also plays your pictures, videos, and music from your computer's local hard drives, optical drives, and from networks. It can then sort them by name, date, tags and other file attributes.

It is well worth exploring this package, but we do not have the space for much more here. To get you going further we suggest you work through the pages on this Web site:

www.microsoft.com/uk/windows/windows-media-center

Fig. 6.27 Getting Started with Windows Media Center

Just click the large buttons on this page and you will soon get started and come to grips with Windows Media Center.

Windows Live Movie Maker

Windows Live Movie Maker is Microsoft's very powerful free program for creating and editing digital videos. Once you have created them you can publish your movies to SkyDrive, Facebook, YouTube, and Windows Live Groups directly from the application.

Although it is not included with Windows 7 this is not a problem as Microsoft has made **Windows Live Essentials** available as a free optional download. This includes a number of new versions of applications designed especially to work with Windows 7, including **Windows Live Movie Maker**. You can download it from the following Web site:

http://explore.live.com/windows-live-movie-maker

Fig. 6.28 Downloading Windows Live Movie Maker

If more exploration is required here you could even look for our book BP710 *An Introduction to Windows Live Essentials* (see page 74).

7

Controlling Your PC

The main way to control your PC is from the **Control Panel**, which provides quick and easy ways to change the hardware and software settings of your system.

Fig. 7.1 Opening the Control Panel

To access the **Control Panel**, click the **Start** button, then left-click the **Control Panel** button on the Start menu, pointed to here in Fig. 7.1.

This opens the Control Panel window in the default **Category** view, shown in Fig. 7.2 on the next page.

From here, you can add new hardware, remove or change programs, change the display type and its resolution, change the printer fonts, change your region and time settings, control your computer's setup and security, change size of the screen font, and change the keyboard repeat rate, etc.

In other words, once you know your way round the Control Panel, you can set up Windows 7 just how you want it.

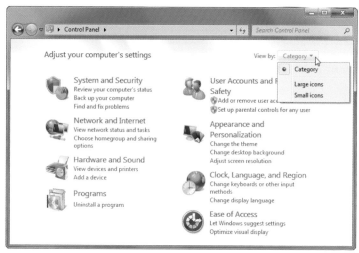

Fig. 7.2 The Windows 7 Control Panel in Category View

Each option, shown above, has a listing below it relevant to that category. Also, note there is the usual **Search** box at the top-right of the window. In Fig. 7.3 we typed **sight** in the **Search** box and what we needed immediately appeared below. This is cool.

Fig. 7.3 Control Panel Search Results

However daunting it may look, it is a very good idea to get familiar with the **Control Panel** features. You may find this easier from the **Large Icons** view, shown in Fig. 7.4 on the next page, which is opened from the **View by** drop-down menu shown open at the top of Fig. 7.2.

Fig. 7.4 The Control Panel in Large Icons View

The actual options available in your **Control Panel** depend on your PC hardware, and your version of Windows 7.

Windows 7 GodMode

 The Control Panel is an essential tool for controlling Windows 7 but sometimes it's not easy to find what you want. There is, however, another little-known way you can adjust the settings on your Windows 7 computer, which gives all the adjustment options in one place. This is the unusually named **GodMode**.

To use your Windows 7 GodMode settings, you first need to create a new folder on your desktop for it. To do this right-click on the desktop and select the **New**, **Folder** options from the context menu. This will add a default folder to your desktop probably named New folder, as shown here.

Next, right-click on the new folder icon and select **Properties** to open the New folder Properties dialogue box. In the General tab type the following code into the text box at the top to change the name of the folder:

GodMode.{ED7BA470-8E54-465E-825C-99712043E01C}

Then click the **OK** button. The folder should have changed from the default blank folder icon to the Control Panel icon shown at the top of the page. Double-clicking this icon opens the GodMode window shown below in Fig. 7.5, with all your Windows 7 adjustments in one place. A very useful tool.

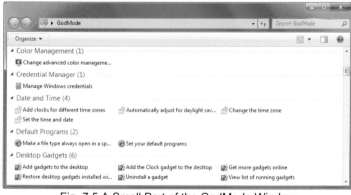

Fig. 7.5 A Small Part of the GodMode Window

Changing your Display

The 3D aspects of Windows 7 require the highest possible screen resolution that your graphics card is capable of delivering. Higher screen resolution gives you better text clarity, sharper images, and more items fit on your screen, in other words you can see more. At lower resolutions, less items fit on the screen, and images may have jagged edges.

For example, a display resolution of 800 × 600 pixels (picture elements) is low, while one of 1600 × 1200 pixels is higher. In general, LCD monitors can support higher resolutions than CRT monitors and whether you can increase your screen resolution depends on the size and capability of your monitor and the type of video card installed in your computer.

To find out if you can increase the display resolution of your computer screen, try the following:

In the **Control Panel** window (Fig. 7.2), click the **Adjust screen resolution** link, in the **Appearance and Personalization** section to open the Display Settings box shown in Fig. 7.6 below.

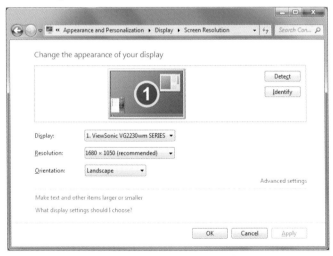

Fig. 7.6 The Display Settings Box

In this box, you can click the **Identify** button to find out the type of display your PC is using or whether an external monitor is connected to your computer. You can also change the **Resolution** and **Orientation** of your screen and make text and icons larger. For these new settings to take effect, click the **Apply** button, but before the new settings are set, you'll be asked to log off, so make sure any work you were doing has been saved! For full details on this press the **F1** key to open the **Help** window on **Getting the best display on your monitor**.

Windows 7 Themes

Next, try clicking the **Change the theme** link in the **Appearance and Personalization** section of the **Control Panel**, to open the window in Fig. 7.7. Or more simply right-click the Desktop and choose **Personalize**.

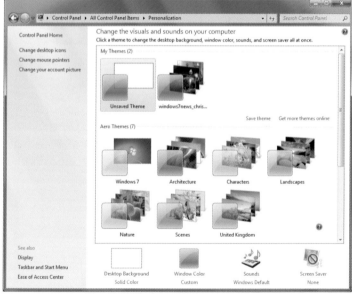

Fig. 7.7 Windows 7 Theme Options

Plenty to explore here. For example, you can change the **Desktop Background**, control the **Window Color**, set the **Sounds** the system makes, or set a **Screen Saver**.

A Windows 7 **Aero Theme** is a combination of desktop background (or wallpaper), Aero glass window colour, sound scheme, and screen saver. Windows 7 comes with a number of built-in Themes that are unique to different regions around the World. Fig. 7.7 for example shows the United Kingdom Aero Theme. You can also create your own Themes if that sort of thing turns you on.

United Kingdom

Other International Themes

When Windows 7 is installed, it asks for your language, time and currency, and installs a suitable theme based on your answers. For the UK it also installs themes from other English-speaking countries – Australia, Canada, South Africa and the USA. These are hidden though, but there is a simple way you can install and use them.

Click the **Start** button 🔵, type the following into the **Search programs and files** box and press the **Enter** key.

C:\Windows\Globalization\MCT

An Explorer window will open with a list of subfolders containing themes for specific countries, as in Fig. 7.8.

Name	Date modified	Type	Size
MCT-AU	14/07/2009 08:54	File folder	
MCT-CA	14/07/2009 08:54	File folder	
MCT-GB	14/07/2009 08:55	File folder	
MCT-US	14/07/2009 08:55	File folder	
MCT-ZA	14/07/2009 08:56	File folder	

Fig. 7.8 Theme Folders for English Speaking Countries

Where AU is for Australia, CA for Canada, GB for Great Britain, US for the United States, and ZA for South Africa.

To use the theme of any of these countries double-click to open its folder, double-click the **Theme** sub-folder and double-click the File there AU   14/07/2009 08:54   Windows Theme File   3 KB. In this case the Australia Theme will be installed in the **My Themes** section of the **Personalization** window (Fig. 7.7).

You can then use them as you would any other theme, or by right-clicking the Desktop, choosing **Personalize**, and then clicking the theme icon, as shown here.

Australia

Background and Colours

If you click the **Desktop Background** button (Fig. 7.7) you can choose multiple background images which cycle through a slide show, as shown in Fig. 7.9.

Fig. 7.9 Creating a Slide Show Background

You can choose from the **Windows Desktop Backgrounds**, or click **Browse** and select your own photos. Bear in mind that the simpler your screen background the easier it is to see your desktop icons, if you use them. Well worth a good play here.

Clicking the **Window Color** link in the **Personalization** window opens the screen in Fig. 7.10 below. If the transparency of the open windows on your desktop is getting on your nerves, just uncheck **Enable transparency**. We also find that the **Color intensity** is best set fairly high on the slider otherwise it is sometimes difficult to see which item in a window is selected.

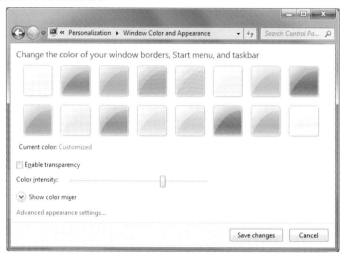

Fig. 7.10 Changing the Colour and Appearance of Windows

Screen Savers

Clicking the **Screen Saver** link in the **Personalization** window opens the screen shown in Fig. 7.11 on the next page.

Clicking the down-arrow on the **Screen saver** box reveals a drop-down menu of the installed screen savers you can choose from. We quite like the **Bubbles** one, which doesn't clear the screen, but drifts a cloud of transparent bubbles over it. Very classy.

Fig. 7.11 Selecting a Screen Saver

On this window you can also change the time of inactivity before the screen saver starts up. With some screen savers, clicking the **Settings** button displays a box for you to control their display settings.

When you make all the changes you want, click the **Preview** button to see the effect of the selected options in full screen. When you are happy, stop the preview, then click the **Apply** button followed by the **OK** button. But don't then spend hours watching your screen saver, unless you've nothing else to do, of course!

Microsoft offers a number of extra Theme Packs on the Windows 7 Web site. To download and install them, click the **Get more themes online** link in the **My Themes** section of the Personalize window (Fig. 7.7).

Controlling Devices and Printers

When your computer was first set up, your devices and printers should have been installed automatically. If not, select **View devices and printers** in the **Hardware and Sound** section of the **Control Panel**, or click the **Start** button ⊕ and choose **Devices and Printers** from the right column of the **Start** menu. Both of these open the **Devices and Printers** window, shown in Fig. 7.12 below.

Fig. 7.12 The Devices and Printers Folder

Our **Devices and Printers** folder displays six devices and seven printers and faxes as shown above. In the case of the printers, two are physical ones for printing to paper and three for creating formatted print documents (**.pdf** and **.xps**).

  With Windows 7, most devices and printers are automatically detected at installation time, or during the boot-up process, called **Plug and Play**. So if you add a new printer or a new device, like a camera, to your system it should be recognised. You may be asked for the necessary driver files if they are not already in the Windows directory, but these come on a CD, or can be found on the manufacturer's Web site.

Configuring your Printer

To control your printer, double-click its icon in the **Devices and Printers** folder (Fig. 7.12), to open a Printer Control window like that shown in Fig. 7.13 below.

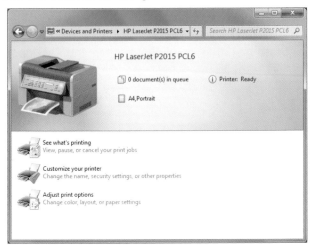

Fig. 7.13 The Printer Control Window

Here in the Printer Window you can control what is waiting to be printed, customise your printer, and set all the printer's parameters, such as the printer port (or network path), paper and graphics options, built-in fonts, and other device options specific to the printer.

A newly installed printer is automatically set as the default printer, indicated by a green tick against ✅ it in the **Devices and Printers** folder. To change the default printer, select a printer connected to your PC, right-click it, and choose the **Set as default printer** option from the drop-down menu.

Once you have installed and configured your printers, the quickest way to print a simple document or file is to print using Windows itself. Locate the file that you want to print in a folder, maybe **Documents**, right-click it, and select **Print**. Windows will print it using your default printer settings.

For more control of the print operation, you should open the document in a program and use its **File**, **Print** menu options.

Managing Print Jobs

If you want to find out what is happening when you have sent documents to your printer, double-click the **See what's printing** option in the Printer Control window, or double-click the printer icon 🖶 in the Notification Area of the Task bar, to open the **Print Queue**.

Fig. 7.14 The Print Queue

This displays detailed information about the work actually being printed, or of print jobs that are waiting in the queue. This includes the name of the document, its status and 'owner', when it was added to the print queue, the printing progress and when printing was started.

You can control the printing operations from the **Printer** and **Document** menu options of the **Print Queue** window. Selecting **Printer**, **Pause Printing** will stop the operation until you make the same selection again. The **Cancel All Documents** option will remove all the print jobs from the queue, but it sometimes takes a while.

Handling Faxes

 Windows 7 ships with a Fax and Scan utility which actually works. The Scan part of the utility has always worked in previous versions of Windows, but for us this is the first version of Windows which successfully addresses Faxes, ironically as they are losing their popularity!

To use the Fax utility, all you have to do is to connect your PC's Fax modem to a telephone line, but remember that if you are on Broadband this connection has to be made via a Broadband filter.

To start the Fax and Scan utility, either double-click the **Fax** icon in the **Devices and Printers** folder, or click the **Start** button then click the **Windows Fax and Scan** entry in the **All Programs** list. Both open the window below.

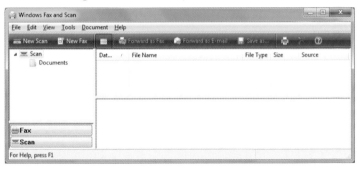

Fig. 7.15 The Opening Fax and Scan Utility Window

As you can see from the opening screen of this utility, you can select either a **New Scan** or a **New Fax**. Clicking the **New Fax** button, opens the window below.

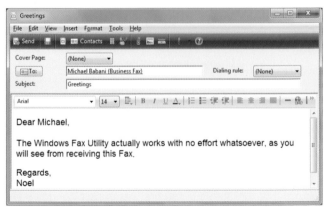

Fig. 7.16 The New Fax Screen

Note that the Fax utility is very similar to an e-mail program. You can select the recipient from your contacts list, provided you have a separate entry for the Fax number, you can attach a file, etc. We find that in terms of readability, the best font size for the body of the Fax is 14 point.

Next, click the **New Scan** button (see Fig. 7.15) to open the first Scan screen in which you can change the Resolution, Brightness and Contrast of your scanner, and Preview or Scan the object in question. Pressing the Scan button, opens the window below.

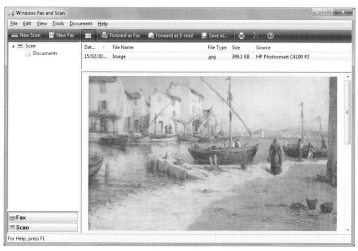

Fig. 7.17 The New Scan Screen

As you can see, you can forward the scan image as a Fax, as an e-mail, or save it. A really wonderful utility!

Working with Programs

Installing programs on your PC is very easy with Windows 7. Just place the CD or DVD that the software came on in the appropriate drive and Windows will start the installation process automatically. If you downloaded the program from the Internet, it should run and install itself.

Clicking the **Programs** section of the **Control Panel** opens the sub-panel shown in Fig. 7.18.

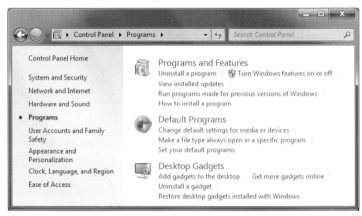

Fig. 7.18 The Programs Section of the Control Panel

Uninstall or Change a Program

Uninstalling programs or changing an already installed one is very easy with Windows. To do either, click the **Uninstall a program** link in the **Programs and Features** section of the **Control Panel**, shown in Fig. 7.18 above, to open a colourful window similar to the one in Fig. 7.19 on the next page. Your contents will not be the same, obviously!

After selecting a program the four options, **Organize**, **Uninstall**, **Change**, and **Repair**, may appear on the toolbar, as shown in Fig. 7.19. With some programs **Change** and/or **Repair** are not available, while with others **Change** is replaced by the **Repair** option.

Using the option to **Uninstall** a program, removes all trace of it from your hard disc, although sometimes the folders are left empty on your hard drive.

Note: Be careful with this application, because double-clicking a program on the list might remove it without further warning!

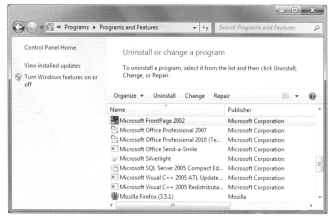

Fig. 7.19 Uninstalling and Changing Programs

Running a Program as Administrator

If a program that you are trying to run gives you errors such as **Access Denied** or **No Permission**, then running it as an administrator can usually give the permission it needs to run properly. With Windows, an administrator is someone allowed to make changes on a computer that will affect other users. These include security settings, installing software and hardware, and being able to access all files on the computer.

Somewhat confusingly even if your account is set up as an Administrator you will still get prompted to give Administrator rights at certain times. There is a 'Hidden Administrator' account with full powers over your computer and this is the one you sometimes have to access.

Warning - You should only allow a program that you trust to run as administrator as once you have given full permission, it will have complete access to your computer.

To temporarily run a program as an administrator (until it is closed again), right-click on the program shortcut or its **.exe** file in a folder list, and select Run as administrator as shown in Fig. 7.20 on the next page. If prompted with a UAC window (see page 194), then click **Yes** to allow the program to run with full permission as an administrator.

Fig. 7.20

If you are doing this while logged in as a standard user instead of an administrator, then you will need to provide the administrator's password before the program will run as administrator.

Some older programs may need to be run in Compatibility Mode, in which case select the **Troubleshoot compatibility** option shown in Fig. 7.20 and follow a simple Wizard procedure.

Windows Features

Some programs and features included with Windows, must be turned on before you can use them, and others such as

Fig. 7.21 Windows Features

Internet Explorer 8, can be turned off. Some are turned on by default, but you can turn them off if you don't need them.

You might not need to make any changes to your Windows 7 features, but if you do, just click the **Turn Windows features on or off** link in the **Programs and Features** section of the **Control Panel** (Fig. 7.18), to open the Windows Features box shown in Fig. 7.21 above. Here you can select the features you want included with Windows by ticking in the boxes.

8

Using E-mail

 Windows 7 does not come packaged with an e-mail program, but Microsoft has made **Windows Live Essentials** available as an optional download. This includes a new version of **Windows Live Mail**, designed to work with Windows 7. Once you have downloaded and installed this, as long as you are connected to the Internet and set up correctly, you can communicate with others by e-mail. Wherever they are in the World, all you need to know is their e-mail address. In this chapter we look at Windows Live Mail, but you can use another program if you prefer.

Windows Live Essentials

Windows Live Mail is Microsoft's excellent all-in-one package for e-mail, contacts management, newsgroups, and feeds. With it you can access several different e-mail accounts from the one window, including Web based accounts from Windows Live Hotmail, MSN Hotmail, AOL, Gmail and premium Yahoo! Accounts. Its PhotoMail feature lets you send large photographs in your messages.

You can obtain **Windows Live** from several Microsoft Web sites, including:

http://explore.live.com/windows-live-essentials

`Download now` Have a good look around and when you are ready click the **Download now** button, select **Run** and **Yes** when asked, choose the components that you want (as in Fig. 8.1) and finally click the **Install** button to download and install them on your PC.

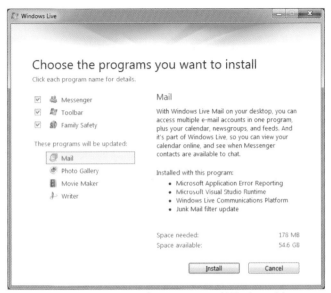

Fig. 8.1 Installing the Components of Windows Live

Windows Live Mail

To start Live Mail, click the **Start** button 🌐 open the **All Programs** menu (see page 21), click **Windows Live**, and then **Windows Live Mail**. As you will probably be using your e-mail program every time you open your PC, perhaps now would be a good time to add it to the **Taskbar**. Then in the future you just need to click its icon to get going.

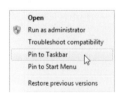

Fig. 8.2
Right-click Menu

This is very easy to do, just right-click the **Windows Live Mail** entry in the **All Programs** menu and select the **Pin to Taskbar** option in the context menu, as shown here in Fig. 8.2. An icon is placed on the right of your Taskbar buttons. You can then drag it to where you want on the bar.

Connecting to your Server

When you run Live Mail for the first time, you are prompted to add an e-mail account. You will need the following information from the supplier of your e-mail service. Your e-mail address and password, the type of e-mail server to be used, and the address of the incoming and outgoing e-mail servers you should use.

If the connection process does not start automatically, use the **Tools**, **Accounts** menu command, click the **Add** button, select **E-mail Account** and click **Next** to start it manually. Follow the instructions from screen to screen. It should only take a minute. You can add all your different e-mail accounts like this and view them all from the same window.

Once your connection is established, opening the **Inbox** will display any messages waiting in your mailbox, as shown in Fig. 8.3 below.

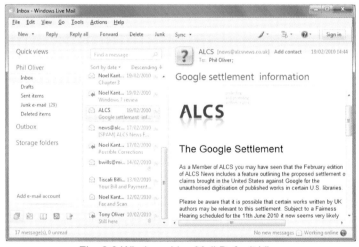

Fig. 8.3 Windows Live Mail Default View

This shows the default layout of the Windows Live Mail window, which consists of the **Folder Pane** on the left, Menu and Tool bars, a **Message List** in the centre below a **Search** box, and a **Reading Pane** on the right with a Message header above it.

The **Folder Pane** contains the active mail folders. Clicking on one of these, displays its contents in the **Message List**. Clicking on a message in the list opens a preview of it in the **Reading Pane**, while double-clicking on a message opens the message in its own window.

To check your mail at any time, click the **Sync** toolbar button 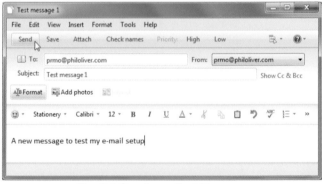 which with a Broadband connection will automatically download your messages. If you are using a Dial-up connection, it will display the Dial-up Connection window, for you to connect to the Internet. Any new messages will then be downloaded from your mailbox.

A Test E-mail Message

Before explaining in more detail the main features of **Windows Live Mail** we will step through the procedure of sending a very simple e-mail message. The best way to test out any unfamiliar e-mail features is to send a test message to your own e-mail address. This saves wasting somebody else's time, and the message can be very quickly checked.

To start, click the **New** button on the toolbar to open the New Message window, shown in Fig. 8.4.

Fig. 8.4 Sending a Test Message

Type your own e-mail address in the **To:** field, and a title for the message in the **Subject:** field. The text in this subject field will form a header for the message when it is received, so it helps to show in a few words what the message is about. Next, type your message in the main body of the window and click the **Send** button Send .

By default, your message is placed in the **Outbox** folder and sent immediately if you are on Broadband, otherwise you will have to press the **Sync** button to send it.

When **Live Mail** next checks for mail, it should find the message and download it into your **Inbox** folder (Fig. 8.7).

The Main Window

Windows Live Mail uses three major windows, which we will refer to as: the Main window which opens first; the Read Message window for reading your mail; and the New Message window, to compose your outgoing mail messages.

The Main window consists of a menu, a toolbar, and three panes described next, with the default display shown in our example in Fig. 8.3. You can choose different pane layouts, and customise the toolbar, by clicking the **Menus** button and choosing the **Layout**, or **Customize Toolbar** options, but we will let you try these for yourself.

The Folders List – This contains a list of your mail folders, and has shortcuts to your **Calendar** , **Contacts** , **Feeds** and **Newsgroups** , and back to **Mail** . Each account has at least five mail folders, as shown in Fig. 8.5 on the next page. You can add your own (usually in the Storage folders section) with the **File**, **Folder**, **Create new folder** command from the Main window. You can then drag messages from the **Message List** and drop them into a folder for storage.

The **Quick views** option at the top lets you view all the unread mail you have received. This is really useful when you have multiple mail accounts open.

If you have problems with space on your screen, you can minimise the **Folders List** to a **Compact** view by dragging its right border to the left (as shown in Fig. 8.5).

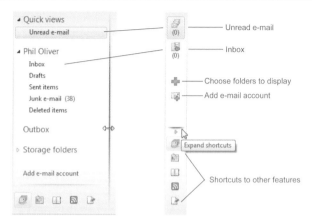

Fig. 8.5 The Default Folders List, in Normal and Compact Views

The Message List – When you select a folder, by clicking it in the **Folders List**, the **Message List** shows the contents of that folder with brief details given for each message, as shown here in Fig. 8.6.

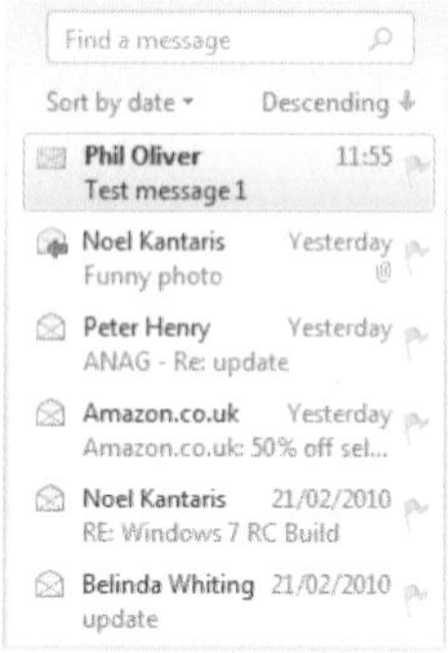

The first column shows a message status icon, with the most common being: Unread ✉, Read ✉, Replied to and Forwarded. Next is the name of the sender and when it arrived. The second row shows the 'Subject' or title of each message followed by status icons showing, for example, if it has an attachment, or has been 'flagged'.

Fig. 8.6 The Message List

You can control how this pane displays by clicking the **Menus** button and choosing the **Layout**, **Message List** menu options.

To sort a list of messages, click the **Sort by ...** link and choose how you want it sorted from the drop-down menu.

To search for a message term in the list, type the term in the **Find a message** box at the top and click the button.

The Reading Pane – When you select a message in the **Message List**, by clicking it once, it is displayed in the **Reading Pane** (to the right by default), which takes up the rest of the window. This lets you read the beginning of the message without actually opening it. If it is worth reading, double-clicking the header in the **Message List**, will open the message in the Read Message window.

The Read Message Window

If you double-click a message in the **Message List** of the Main window, the Read Message window is opened as shown in Fig. 8.7 below.

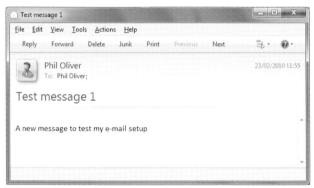

Fig. 8.7 Our Test Message in the Read Message Window

This is the best window to read your mail in. It has its own menu system and self-explanatory toolbar, and lets you rapidly process and move between the messages in a folder.

Windows Live Mail has an automated junk filter which scans incoming messages and automatically moves them to the junk folder if it identifies them as spam or a phishing attack. If a message gets through that you don't like, just clicking the **Junk** button Junk will do the same thing. You should make a habit of checking the **Junk e-mail** folder(s) every now and then, as some messages may be put there by mistake. If that happens just clicking the **Not junk** button Not junk will move the message to your **Inbox**.

The New Message Window

Clicking the **New** button 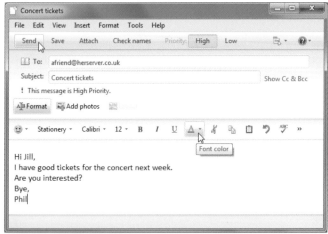 on the Main Window toolbar opens the New Message window, shown in Fig. 8.8. This is where you create your e-mail messages in Live Mail. It is important to understand its features, so that you can get the most out of it.

Fig. 8.8 The New Message Window

The toolbar icons in this window are all self-explanatory, but if necessary, hovering the pointer over one will tell you what it does.

Message Formatting

Windows Live Mail provides quite sophisticated formatting options for an e-mail editor from both the **Format** menu and the Format toolbar. These only work if you prepare the message in HTML format, as used in Web documents. You can set this to be your default mail sending format using the Send tab in the **Tools**, **Options** box of the **Main Window**.

The **Format** toolbar shown open in Fig. 8.8 above is added to the New Message window when you are in HTML mode and all the **Format** menu options are then made active.

Photo E-mails

You can add photos to e-mail messages in two ways, as attachments (described next), or in a photo e-mail. With a photo e-mail, as long as you are signed in to Windows Live Mail with a Windows Live ID (using the e-mail address and password that you use to sign in to all Windows Live services, as described on page 131), you can upload the full versions of your photos and save them on Windows' servers. Only thumbnails of them will be placed in your message, so your e-mail will be smaller and quicker to send, but the recipient will be able to view or download the full photos.

To create a photo e-mail, click the **New** button  to open the New Message window, shown earlier in Fig. 8.4, and prepare your message as normal. Click where you want to insert photos in the message and then click the **Add photos** button. Select the photos you want to send followed by the **Add** button, and click **Done** to finish.

Fig. 8.9 Thumbnails in a Photo E-mail

To format your message, you click to format the text, to add photo frames or more photos, and to set the message layout, as shown in Fig. 8.9 above. Finally click the **Send** button to send your Photo e-mail. This really is well worth doing.

E-mail Attachments

To add an attachment to an e-mail message, such as a photo or work file, you simply click the **Attach** button 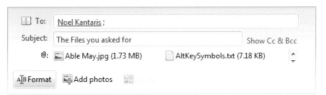 in the New Message window, select the file(s), you want to go with your message, and click **Open**.

Fig. 8.10 Two Attachments Ready to Send

In **Windows Live Mail** the attached files are placed below the **Subject** box. In Fig. 8.10 we show two attachments with their icons telling the recipient what each file is; a graphics (**.jpg**) file and a Notepad (**.txt**) text file in our case. Finally click the **Send** button to send your e-mail.

Receiving Attachments

Fig. 8.11, on the facing page, shows an e-mail we received with three attachments in a Read Message window.

The received message shows the graphics (**.jpg**) file open at the bottom of the window, and all three attachments in the Header bar with icons indicating what type of files they are.

Right-clicking an attachment opens a drop-down menu as shown in Fig. 8.11. From this you can choose to open, print or save the attached files. The **Save all** option is the one most often used.

Double-clicking an attached file icon opens a Mail Attachment window showing you the type of document and asking whether you want to open it. A graphics file (**.jpg**) then opens in **Windows Live Photo Gallery**, and a Word document file opens in Microsoft Word.

As long as you have the necessary programs, each attached file can be opened in situ or saved to disc from within the application that opened it.

Fig. 8.11 Received Attachments in a Read Message Window

Replying to a Message

When you receive an e-mail message that you want to reply to, Live Mail makes it very easy to do.

With the message you want to reply to open, click the **Reply** button Reply to open the New Message window. The reply address and the subject field are both filled in automatically for you, and the text of the message you are replying to will, by default, be placed under the insertion point.

You can edit this text, so that it is obvious what you are referring to. Just a few lines may well be enough. Then type your reply, format whatever you want and click the **Send** button Send .

Deleting Messages

Some e-mail messages you receive will be worth keeping, but most will need deleting. From the Read Message window you just click the **Delete** button [Delete] to do this. From the Main window you can select the messages you don't want to keep in the **Messages List** and either, click the **Delete** button [Delete], or press the **Delete** key.

Whenever you delete a message it is actually moved to the **Deleted Items** folder. If ignored, this folder gets bigger and bigger over time, so you need to check it frequently and manually re-delete messages you will not need again.

To get this done automatically, you use the **Tools**, **Options** menu command to open the Options dialogue box, click the Advanced tab and click the **Maintenance** button at the bottom of the screen and check the **Empty messages from the 'Deleted Items' folder on exit** box in the displayed Maintenance screen. Your deletions will then be fully removed whenever you close Windows Live Mail.

Spell Checking Messages

Just because e-mail messages are a quick way of getting in touch with friends and family, there is no reason why they should be full of spelling mistakes, as Windows Live Mail has a good spelling checker built in.

Fig. 8.12 Correcting
Spelling Mistakes

To try it out, prepare a message in the New Message window, but with obvious spelling mistakes, maybe like ours. Errors will be underlined in red, as shown in Fig. 8.12.

Right-clicking a flagged 'error' opens a drop-down menu. You can accept one of the suggestions, **Ignore All** occurrences in the message, or add your original word to the dictionary for future use. This works very well.

Printing Messages

Windows Live Mail lets you print e-mail messages to paper, but it doesn't give you any control over the page settings it uses. When you are ready to print a message, if it is open in the Read Message window, click the **Print** button `Print`. In the **Message List** use the **Ctrl+P** key combination, or the **File**, **Print** menu command. All of these open the standard Windows Print dialogue box which allows you to select one of your printers, the **Page Range**, and **Number of copies** you want. Clicking the **Print** button will start the process.

Fig. 8.13 The Windows Print Dialogue Box

The Contacts Folder

Windows Live Mail lets you create and keep a contact list to store details such as the names, addresses, phone numbers, and e-mail addresses of your contacts, or people you communicate with most.

If you have never signed in to Live Mail with a Windows Live ID (page 131), your contact list will contain only the contacts you have added or imported into the program. If you are signed in, Live Mail uses the contact list associated with your Windows Live ID and any changes that you make to your contacts in Live Mail will be saved and also used in Windows Live Messenger, Windows Live Hotmail, and other Windows Live products and services.

In Live Mail you click the **Contacts** button ▥ at the bottom of the **Folder Pane** to access the **Contacts** window.

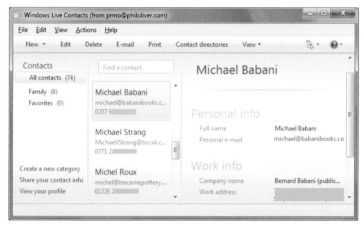

Fig. 8.14 The Live Mail Contacts Window

Here in Fig. 8.14 we show a small part of a **Contacts** folder. You can add a person's details in the **Add a Contact** box opened by clicking the **New** button New ▾ , as shown in Fig. 8.15 on the facing page.

Use the Contact tab to enter the name, phone, and e-mail details for your new contact. The Personal tab screen is used to enter their personal address, phone and fax numbers, and Web site. You can also enter similar information for Work.

The rest of the information can be entered if you have the time, or be entered later by editing the Contact's entry.

Unfortunately, there does not seem to be any facility for adding photos of your contacts, as in earlier versions.

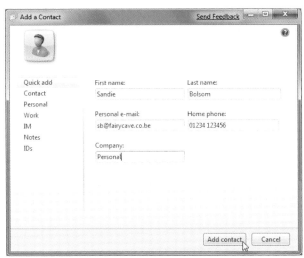

Fig. 8.15 The Add a Contact Window

To send a new message from your **Contacts** list, highlight their name and click the **E-mail** button E-mail to open a pre-addressed New Message window in Live Mail.

Or, from the New Message window, start typing a name in the ⊞ To: box and select from the options presented, or click on the ⊞ To: button, or use the **Tools**, **Select from contacts** command, to open the **Send an E-mail** box.

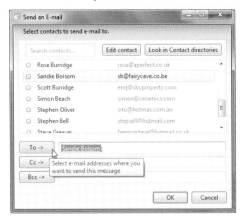

Fig. 8.16
Selecting a Contact

In this box, you can select a person's name and click either the **To:** button to place it in the **To** field of your message, the **Cc:** button to place it in the **Copy** field, or the **Bcc:** button to place it in the **Blind Copy** field (so that the address will not be visible to the main recipient of the message).

The Windows Calendar

Windows Live Mail also provides you with a calendar which is opened by clicking the **Calendar** button 📅 at the bottom of the **Folder Pane**.

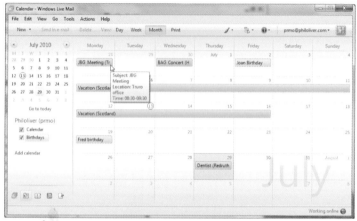

Fig. 8.17 The Live Mail Calendar

This will provide you with all the scheduling tools you should ever need. It provides day, week and month views, and supports multiple, colour-coded calendars, making it easy to keep schedules for work, family, school and hobbies, etc.

We will leave it to you to explore this excellent facility on your own.

Getting Help

As you would expect, Live Mail has a **Help** system if you want to go deeper. It is opened in an Internet Explorer window by clicking the **Help** button , pressing the **F1** function key, or clicking the **Help** Menu bar option and selecting **Get Help with Mail** from the drop-down menu. All of these open the screen shown in Fig. 8.18 below.

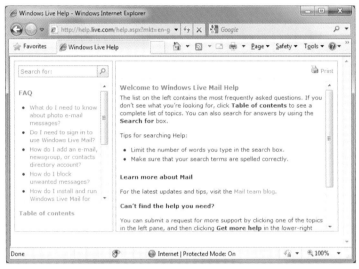

Fig. 8.18 Help with Windows Live Mail

Windows Live ID

You don't have to sign in with a Windows Live ID to use Windows Live Mail, but if you do, you can connect to other Windows Live services and use extra features of Live Mail. When you are signed in, Live Mail uses the contact list and calendars associated with your Windows Live ID and keeps them synchronised for you automatically.

To sign in to Windows Live ID from Live Mail, click the **Sign in** button Sign in in the upper-right corner of the Live Mail Main window (see Fig. 8.3).

Fig. 8.19 Signing in to Windows Live ID

If you have them, type your Windows Live ID and password, into the boxes shown above and click **Sign in**. If not, click the **Don't have a Windows Live ID?** link, and then follow the on-screen instructions to sign up. It really doesn't take very long to get one.

If you tick the **Remember my password** check box, you won't have to remember it again in the future. But of course, you should only do this on your own personal computer.

Once you have signed in the procedure is automatic whenever you open Windows Live Mail. To sign out again, use the **Tools**, **Options** menu command and click the **Stop signing in** button on the Connection tab sheet shown in Fig. 8.20 below.

Fig. 8.20 Signing out of Windows Live ID

9

Exploring the Internet

The Internet links many millions of computers around the world and has revolutionised how we get information and use our computers. How did we ever manage without it? Amongst the many facilities available are browsing the Web and using e-mail to keep in contact with family and friends.

Once you are connected to the Internet you can send e-mail messages to anyone with an e-mail address anywhere in the world. Its free and almost instant. No wonder it's so popular. If you are like us, almost the first thing you do every day is check your e-mail!

The Web (or World Wide Web to use its full name) consists of millions of web sites which give a magazine-like view of almost everything you can think of, but with sound and video as well.

You view the Web with a Web browser, and when Windows 7 is first installed, Microsoft's Internet Explorer 8 is installed with it. That is what we will briefly cover in this chapter, but you can install and use another Web browsing program if you prefer (page 135).

Internet Explorer 8

 To start **Internet Explorer**, either click its icon on the **Taskbar** 🅔, or click **Start**, **All Programs**, and select **Internet Explorer** 🌐 Internet Explorer from the **Start** menu. Either of these options, opens Microsoft's Internet browser. The first time you do this, you may be stepped through the process of establishing a connection to the Internet.

There are three ways of doing this; **Wireless**, **Broadband**, or **Dial-up**. For a **Wireless** connection you need a wireless router or a network. For a **Broadband** connection you need a broadband modem, also called DSL (Digital Subscriber Line), or a cable modem. For the slowest option, a **Dial-up** connection, you will need a modem. We think most people these days use a wireless router.

Fig. 9.1 Starting Connection Setup

Whichever method you select you will need to subscribe to an Internet Service Provider (ISP) and you might have to purchase additional hardware. Normally, ISPs provide you with a CD which automates the setup process, but you could also use the **Tools** toolbar icon in Internet Explorer. Select **Internet Options** from the drop-down menu and click the **Setup** button on the Connections tab sheet, as shown here in Fig. 9.1.

However, before starting this operation be sure to find out from your ISP, exactly what settings you will need to enter. They usually send you a letter or e-mail with these details.

The first time you manage to access the Web you will probably get a page supplied by Microsoft or your Service Provider. But you can control what Web page is displayed when you start **Explorer** (called your Home page), in the **General** settings sheet opened with the **Tools**, **Internet Options** menu command. Select **Use current** to make any currently open pages your home pages, or **Use blank** to show a clear window whenever you start **Explorer**.

Browser Choice Update

Microsoft have had a long standing, and in our view ridiculous, dispute with the European Commission because it bundles the Explorer browser with its Windows operating systems. This was recently resolved and to comply with the legal settlement Microsoft is required to inform customers who currently use Internet Explorer as their default browser that there are other web browser choices available.

 So if you are using Windows 7, and have your regional settings set to the United Kingdom or another European country you have probably received the Browser Choice update through the Windows Update service. Once installed, if Internet Explorer is your default web browser, it will place a shortcut for the Browser Choice update on your Desktop, remove the Internet Explorer shortcut from your Taskbar and open the following Browser Choice information window.

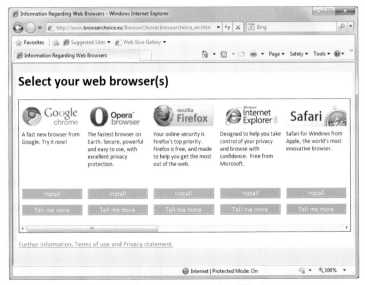

Fig. 9.2 The Browser Choice Window

No need to be afraid of this, it simply lets you choose between twelve browsers (including Explorer 8), many of which we have never even heard of!

To keep Explorer 8 as your browser of choice, click the **Close** button ▬ x ▬ to close the Browser Choice window, and from the **Start** menu choose to pin Explorer 8 back on your Taskbar (see page 116). If you like you can also delete the Browser Choice shortcut from your Desktop, by selecting it and pressing the **Delete** key. You should not be bothered again, and can carry on with this chapter.

If you are interested in the other browsers, click **Tell me more** to get information about them, or click **Install** and follow any on-screen instructions to install any of the browsers you choose.

Searching the Web

There are many millions of Web pages to look at on the Web, so where do you start? One of our favourite places is Google, so let's take a quick look.

Start **Explorer**, if it is not already going, log onto the Internet (this is done automatically with broadband), then type **www.google.co.uk** into the **Address** bar (see Fig. 9.3), and press the **Enter** key on the keyboard, or click the **Go to** button ➜ to the right of the address bar.

If all is well and your connection is good you should see Google UK's search page, as in Fig. 9.3. Bear in mind that this (and other Web site screens in the book) may be different at the time you access them. Google especially, like to change their opening logos often and particularly for special events.

Moving the mouse over the underlined links, and some graphics on the page, changes the pointer to a hand 🖑. Clicking the hand pointer, jumps you to different parts of the Web site, or to other sites. This is how the Web works.

Fig. 9.3 The Google UK Search Page

Just type some text that you would like information on into the large text box and click the **Google Search** button to get going. Where you stop is up to you!

The Address and Status Bars

In Internet Explorer the Address Bar is where you type, or paste, the address or URL of a Web page you want to open.

Fig. 9.4 The Address Bar

This will open one of our personal Web pages when the **Go to** button → is clicked. Note that the **Go to** button then changes to the **Refresh** button ↻ which reloads the Web page shown in the **Address** bar when it is clicked.

Fig. 9.5 Drop-down Menu

The **Address** bar is the main way of opening new Web pages when you know their URLs (Uniform Resource Locator, a fancy term for Web page address). A drop-down menu of the most recent locations you have entered, can be opened by clicking the black down-arrow **Autocomplete** button at the right of the address box.

The address bar also gives you an indication of the security rating of the site you are visiting. When visiting a secure site (your bank for instance) the Security Report 🔒 'padlock' button should be displayed to the right of the site address. Clicking this will identify the site.

When visiting a secure site that has an Extended Validation Certificate the whole Address bar turns green, as shown here 🔒 https://www.paypal.com/uk/cgi-bin/ ▼ PayPal, Inc. [US] ✦ ✕ for the PayPal site.

The **Status** bar, at the bottom of the screen (Fig. 9.6), shows the loading progress of the selected Web page. The URL of the specific Web page appears momentarily, but is then replaced by the green loading progress bar.

Clicking the down-arrow at the extreme right of the **Status** bar opens a menu of zoom options, as shown in the composite screen dump below.

Fig. 9.6 The Status Bar

Explorer Buttons

As with other Windows 7 windows, **Internet Explorer** is fully equipped with toolbars, which have buttons you can left-click to quickly carry out a program function.

Fig. 9.7 The Internet Explorer Address Bar and Toolbars

As you can see, there are several toolbars below the Address bar, which can be switched off if you don't need them by clicking the **Tools** button on the Command Bar (below the Menu Bar) and selecting **Toolbars**, which opens the sub-menu shown in Fig. 9.8. With the **Customize**, **Add or Remove Commands** option you can control what buttons display on the Command Bar, by adding or removing them in the **Customize Toolbar** box, shown in Fig. 9.9 below. From here you can not only **Add** or **Remove** buttons, but you can also rearrange their position on the bar.

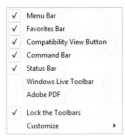

Fig. 9.8   Toolbars

Fig. 9.9 The Customize Toolbar Box

Most of the buttons on the Address bar and other toolbars are pretty self-explanatory. Those on the Address bar have the following functions:

Button		*Function*
	Back	Displays the previous page viewed. If there isn't one this is 'greyed out'.
	Forward	Displays the next page on the **History** list.
	Recent	Opens a drop-down menu of recent pages you have visited.
	Compatibility	Improves the display of Web sites designed for older browsers.
	Refresh	Brings a fresh copy of the current Web page to the viewer.
	Stop	Halts any on-line transfer of page data.
	Search	Searches for the text typed into the **Search** box. You can choose which search engine to use as a default by clicking the down-arrow to the right of the search box.

The Menu bar is located below the Address Bar. You can close this if you don't want it to display (see Fig. 9.7).

The Command Bar, below the Menu Bar has the following default buttons, but you can add more (see Fig. 9.9):

Button		*Function*
	Home	Displays your specified home page, with a Microsoft page as the default.
	Feeds	View Feeds on the open Web site. If a feed is not detected the colour of the icon remains grey.
	Read Mail	Opens your mail client so that you can read your e-mail messages.

	Print	Prints the open Web page, or frame, using the current print settings.
Page ▾		Opens a menu that allows you to open a new window, save the current page, send it or a link to it by e-mail to a recipient, zoom the page, or change the text size on it.
Safety ▾		Displays a drop-down menu that allows you to delete the browsing **History**, Browse in private, see the privacy policy of Web pages, turn on the SmartScreen Filter so that unsafe Web sites can be reported, and activate Windows Update.
Tools ▾		Displays a drop-down menu that allows you to diagnose connection problems, reopen the last browsing session, manage pop-ups, specify your Internet options, and generally control how Explorer works.
	Help	Opens a drop-down menu giving quick access to **Help** topics.
	Blog This	Opens Windows Live Writer to create or add content to your blog.
	Research	Allows you to carry out research into a specific subject.

The Favorites Bar has the following buttons:

Button	*Function*
☆ Favorites	Opens the **Favorites Center** from which you can choose the **Favorites**, **Feeds** or **History** bars.
Add to	Adds a favourite site to the **Favorites** bar.

In addition, there are links to suggested Microsoft Web sites.

Favorites

Using Favorites, or Bookmarks, is an easy way to save Web page addresses for future use. It's much easier to select a

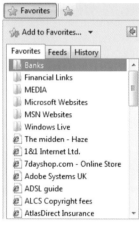

page from a sorted list, than to manually type a URL address into the Address field. You don't have to remember the address and are less likely to make a typing error!

With **Internet Explorer** your Favorites are kept in the **Favorites Center**, shown in Fig. 9.10, opened by clicking ⭐ Favorites , the **Favorites** button.

To keep the list open in a separate pane, you click the **Pin the Favorites Center** button 🔲. To close it again, click its **Close** button ✖.

Fig. 9.10 Favorites

Adding a Favorite – There are several ways to add a 'Favorite' to your list. When you are viewing a Web page that you want to visit again, right-click in the page and select **Add to Favorites** from the context menu. Another way is to click the **Add to Favorites** button ✨ and select the **Add to Favorites** menu option, or you can use the **Ctrl+D** shortcut.

All of these methods open the Add a Favorite dialogue box (Fig. 9.11) in which you can give the new Favorite a name, and choose a folder to put it in. Then just click the **Add** button to finish.

Fig. 9.11 The Add a Favorite Box

Browsing History

Internet Explorer stores details of all the Web pages and files you view on your hard disc, and places temporary

pointers to them in a folder. To return to these in the future, click the **View History** tab in the **Favorites Center**, to open the **History** list shown in Fig. 9.12.

Fig. 9.12 Web Browsing History

In this list you can see what Web sites you visited in the last 3 weeks. Clicking a listed site opens links to the individual Web pages you went to. Clicking any of these will open the page again.

The length of time history items are kept on your hard disc can be set by clicking the **Tools** button and selecting **Internet Options** to open the tabbed dialogue box shown in Fig. 9.13.

Clicking the **Settings** button in the **Browsing history** section, pointed to here, opens an additional dialogue box in which you can select the number of days that **History** files are kept (between 0 and 999). To delete all history items click the **Delete** button, which will release the hard disc space used.

Fig. 9.13 General Internet Options

Web Feeds

Web feeds (feeds for short) are usually used for news and blogs and contain frequently updated content published by a Web site. You can use feeds if you want updates to a Web site to be automatically downloaded to your PC.

When you visit a Web page that contains feeds, the grey **Feeds** button  on the Internet Explorer toolbar changes to orange . To look at the feeds, click the feed symbol . To get content automatically downloaded to your computer, you will need to subscribe to the feed. This is very easy to do, and doesn't cost anything! Just clicking a **Subscribe to this feed** link, like that shown in Fig. 9.14, opens the **Subscribe to this Feed** box shown in Fig. 9.15. Clicking the **Subscribe** button adds the feed to the 'Common Feed List' in the

Fig. 9.14 Subscribing to a Web Feed

Fig. 9.15 Subscribe to this Feed Box

Favorites Center, and updated information from the feed will be automatically downloaded to your computer for viewing in Internet Explorer.

All your subscribed feeds will be listed in the **Feeds** section of the **Favorites Center**.

Fig. 9.16 Feeds List

Clicking an item in the Feeds list, shown in Fig. 9.16, will open it in the main Explorer pane so you can keep up to date. We use this feature to try to keep ourselves up to date.

Tabbed Browsing

With tabbed browsing you can open several Web sites in one Explorer window each in its own tab, and switch between them by clicking on their tab. To create a new tab, click the **New Tab** icon, pointed to in Fig. 9.17, immediately to the right of the existing tabs.

Fig. 9.17 Creating a New Tab

The first time you do this a special tabbed browsing information page opens as shown in Fig. 9.18 below.

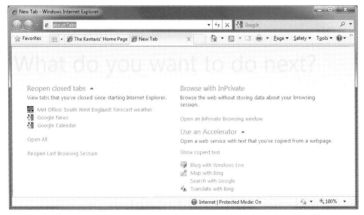

Fig. 9.18 The What Do you Want to Do Next Tabbed Browsing Page

Please read the above text, and note that the 'link' **about:Tabs** is highlighted in the Address Bar so you can simply type a new Web address, or click the **Favorites** button and open one of your **Favorites**.

Explorer 8 has an **InPrivate** browsing mode opened by clicking the **Browse with InPrivate** link shown above. This opens a new window with in the Address Bar. You can then safely browse without leaving any traces. Just closing the InPrivate window returns you to standard mode.

Using Quick Tabs – When you have several Web sites open in different tabs a new button appears to the left of the first tab. This is the **Quick Tabs** button ⊞ which displays all the tabbed Web sites as thumbnail images when it is clicked, as shown in Fig. 9.19.

Fig. 9.19 Using Quick Tabs

In this view you can click a thumbnail to open its Web page, or click the **Close Tab** button ⊠ on a thumbnail to close it. Clicking the **Quick Tabs** button again closes the thumbnails and opens the last Web page you were viewing.

Saving and Opening a Group of Tabs – To save a group of tabs so that you can open the pages again, do the following: Open the Web sites you want to save, maybe ones with a common theme. Click the **Favorites** button ⭐ Favorites to open the Favorites Center, then click the down-arrow by the **Add to Favorites** button, and select **Add Current Tabs to Favorites** from the drop-down list.

In the displayed dialogue box give a name to the folder to contain the selected Web sites – we called it **Best Buys**, (Fig. 9.20) and click the **Add** button.

Fig. 9.20 The Add Tabs to Favorites Box

To open a group of tabs, click the **Favorites** button , select the group folder you want to open (see Fig. 9.21), and either click the arrow to the right of the folder name 🡒 to open all the tabbed sites in the group, or click the folder to display all the Web sites in it and select one of them.

Fig. 9.21 Opening a Group of Tabs

Compatibility Mode

You may find that Internet Explorer 8 does not render some older Web pages correctly. One of our online banking sites for example has some problems with pagination. To resolve these types of problem, just click the **Compatibility View** button 🖼 at the right end of the Address Bar. This displays the Web site as it would be if viewed in Internet Explorer 7, and usually corrects display problems like misaligned text, images, or text boxes.

This only affects the Web site that was active when you pressed the **Compatibility View** button, other sites open at the same time will still use Explorer 8 functionality.

The **Compatibility View** button 🖼 only seems to appear on the Address Bar when it may be needed, so as time goes by and Web developers bring their sites up to 'scratch' you probably won't see it very often!

Internet Explorer Help

That's all we have space for on **Internet Explorer**, but don't forget the built-in **Help** system if you want to go deeper. It is accessed by pressing the **F1** function key, clicking the **Help** button 🔵▾ on the command bar, or clicking the **Help** Menu bar option and selecting **Internet Explorer Help** from the drop-down menu. Any of these open the screen shown in Fig. 9.22 below.

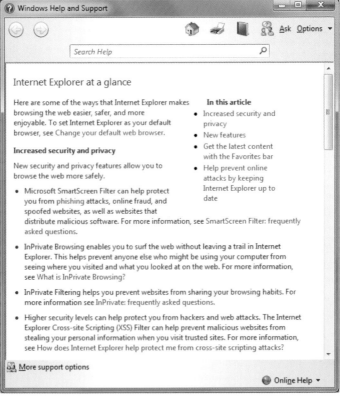

Fig. 9.22 Help on Windows Explorer 8

10

Networks and HomeGroups

 If like many homes and small offices you have several computers, you probably want to be able to network them, or connect them together, so that you can access the Internet from them all, share documents, pictures or music, and print to a single printer. Windows 7 makes this process very much easier than with older versions of Windows. Especially, as we shall see, if all the computers are running under Windows 7.

Network Technologies

The most common types of networks are:

Wireless   These use radio waves to send data between computers. They don't need cables and are usually easier to install than Ethernet, but are often slower, and can be affected by interference from walls, metal objects, and pipes.

Ethernet   These use cables to send data between computers. They are fast, but are more cumbersome and harder to set up.

HomePNA   These use existing home telephone wires to send information between computers.

Powerline   These use existing home electrical wiring to transmit information between computers.

We think the majority of homes use wireless (or Wi-Fi) connections so have only covered that type here.

A Wireless Network

To set up a wireless network each computer to be included needs a Wireless network adaptor. These days laptops almost always have these built in. With a desktop PC a network adaptor can be connected to the USB port or installed inside in an expansion slot.

Fig. 10.1 An
ADSL Router

You will also need a **Wireless Router** to allow access to the Internet and to 'connect' your networked computers. Your Internet Service Provider (ISP) will often offer an ADSL or combination modem/wireless router as part of your broadband package. If not they are easily available online, or at a computer store. Once you have obtained and installed all this necessary hardware and read all the literature that came with it and from your ISP you run the **Set up a new network** wizard. You do this from the main computer that is attached to the router.

First open the Network and Sharing Center by clicking the **Start** button 🏵 on the left of the Taskbar to open the **Start** menu, and type '**network**' into the **Search programs and files** box shown here. Before you have entered the first few letters the ⚏ Network and Sharing Center option will appear in the results list. Just click this.

The Network and Sharing Center that opens (Fig. 10.2) is the control window where you handle all your networking settings and tasks in Windows 7. To open it in the future click on the network icon on the right side of the Taskbar, 🖳 or ▄ill, and select **Open Network and Sharing Center**.

To continue, click the **Set up a new connection or network** link in the right pane and then select the **Set up a new network. Configure a new router or access point** option in the window that opens.

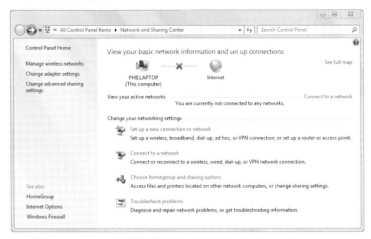

Fig. 10.2 The Network and Sharing Center

The wizard will walk you through the process of adding other computers and devices to the network. If you need more information here we suggest you go to Microsoft's Web site:

http://windows.microsoft.com

and search for **setting up a home network**.

Connecting to a Network

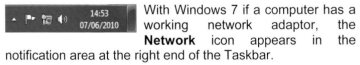

With Windows 7 if a computer has a working network adaptor, the **Network** icon appears in the notification area at the right end of the Taskbar.

This icon indicates whether your network adaptor is an Ethernet adaptor ▦ or a wireless adaptor ⠿. With the wireless connection icon the number of bars indicates the signal strength, with 5 being the strongest. When the computer is not connected to a network, an x shows on the connection icon ▦, while it is connecting it shows as ▦. When a wireless connection is available, the icon has a starburst ▦.

When you physically connect your computer to a network with an Ethernet cable, Windows 7 automatically creates the network connection, but to connect to a wireless network for the first time, you need to make the connection yourself.

Fig. 10.3 An Available Wireless Connection

To do this, click the available wireless connection icon  in the notification area of the taskbar to open a list of available connections as shown here in Fig. 10.3.

The icon adjacent to each available connection (one in our case) indicates its signal strength. Pretty good here, but our Laptop was right next to the Router!

If you hover the pointer over an available network connection a screen tip displays information about the connection as shown on the right for one of ours.

```
Name: DLINK_WIRELESS
Signal Strength: Excellent
Security Type: WEP
Radio Type: 802.11g
SSID: DLINK_WIRELESS
```

Click the connection you want to connect to, and then click the **Connect** button that appears. If a WEP key or WPA password is required, you will be prompted to enter it, and then Windows will connect to the selected network.

Wireless Network Security

For very obvious reasons, when you set up a wireless network you should set it up so that only people you choose can access it. There are several wireless network security systems available.

WPA (Wi-Fi Protected Access) encrypts information, checks to make sure that the network security key has not been modified and also authenticates users to help ensure that only authorised people can access the network.

WEP (Wired Equivalent Privacy) is an older network security method that is still available to support older devices. It uses a network security key which encrypts the information sent across your network. However, WEP security is relatively easy to break and is not recommended on its own.

Also 802.1x authentication can help enhance security for 802.11 type wireless networks and wired Ethernet networks. It can work with WPA or WEP keys and uses an authentication server to validate users and provide network access. This is used mainly in company networks.

Network Locations

A network location in Windows 7 is one of three profiles, Home, Work or Public, which has a collection of network and sharing settings that are applied to the network you are connected to. Depending on the network location assigned to your active network connection, features such as file and printer sharing might be turned on or off automatically.

These network locations are especially useful if you are very mobile and connect your Laptop to different networks. You could use it at home, then connect to your company network in the day, to a friend's network in the evening and to a public network maybe in a hotel during the weekend. Each time you connect to a new network, Windows 7 will assign a network profile, so with one choice you get the entire set of network settings correctly changed.

Home Only choose this location when you are connected to your home network or a network with people and devices you fully trust. By default, network discovery will be turned on and you will be able to see other computers and devices which are part of the network. Also, this will allow other computers from the network to access your computer. On home networks you will also be allowed to create or join a HomeGroup.

Work   Use this when connecting to your workplace network. This profile shares the same settings as a Home network, but it won't allow you to create or join a HomeGroup.

Public   Use this setting when you are in a public place like an airport, hotel, cafe or pub. Network discovery and sharing are turned off and other computers in the network will not be able to access or see yours.

At any time you can change your active Network Location in the **Network and Sharing Center** (page 150) by clicking the link under **View your active networks**.

View your active networks

Network
Home network

Fig. 10.4 Manually Selecting a Network Location

HomeGroups

 A HomeGroup is a new feature in Windows 7 which simplifies the whole network procedure. It allows all your home computers, with Home network location settings, to easily connect and share their content **as long as they are running under Windows 7**.

All your Windows 7 computers in the same HomeGroup can share libraries, folders, files, devices and media without ever having to type passwords whenever anything is accessed. You select what you want shared on each computer and as long as it is 'awake' it can be accessed from the other computers in the group with just a few clicks.

When you first install Windows 7, or set up a new network, you are prompted to select a location type (page 153). When you select Home Network, you are asked if you want to create a HomeGroup.

You can create one at any time, though, in the Network and Sharing Center (see page 150 if you can't remember how to open this).

Fig. 10.5 Ready to Create a New HomeGroup

In the **View your active networks** section you can see the name and type of the network you are connected to, the type of connection and whether you are in a HomeGroup. Fig. 10.5 shows **HomeGroup: Ready to create**.

Clicking the **HomeGroup** link, pointed to in Fig. 10.5 opens the **HomeGroup** window of Fig. 10.6, and the **Create a homegroup** button starts the procedure shown in Fig 10.7.

Fig. 10.6 The HomeGroup Window

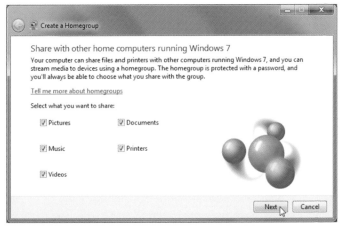

Fig. 10.7 The First HomeGroup Wizard Window

Here you can select what you want to share from a list of your default libraries (Pictures, Documents, Music and Videos) and your printers. Check the items you want to share and click on **Next** to go to the last Wizard window.

Fig. 10.8 Your HomeGroup Password

After a few seconds, Windows 7 will show you the automatically generated password of the HomeGroup, as shown in Fig. 10.8 above. If you will be changing this, just click on **Finish**. If you decide to keep it, then write it down carefully or print it using the link below. You will need an active password when you come to add your other computers to the HomeGroup. Then click on **Finish**.

You are returned to the HomeGroup window of Fig. 10.9, which gives a list of settings and available actions.

To change the HomeGroup password, before adding any other computers to the group, click the **Change the password** link. Click **Change password** in the next box and type your chosen password to replace the new automatically generated one. Make sure it is at least eight characters long. When you are happy, click the **Next** button to complete the action.

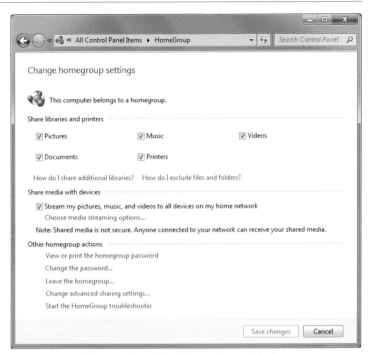

Fig. 10.9 The Final HomeGroup Window

If you ever need the HomeGroup password in the future it is easy to access. Go to the HomeGroup window of any of the computers in the HomeGroup, and click on the **View or print the homegroup password** link (Fig. 10.9).

Adding a PC to the HomeGroup

Once your HomeGroup is created you can join your other home computers to it. On each one, open the **Network and Sharing Center**, and the **View your active networks** section should show **HomeGroup: Available to join**.

Clicking the **HomeGroup** link, opens the **HomeGroup** window of Fig. 10.10, which should tell you there is a HomeGroup available on the network. Clicking the **Join now** button starts the Wizard process as in the last section.

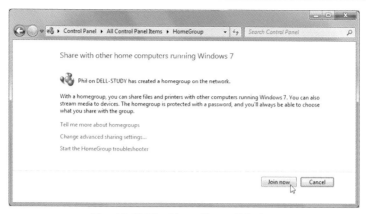

Fig. 10.10 The HomeGroup Window

In the next Wizard window select what libraries and devices you want to share and click the **Next** button. Then, type the HomeGroup password where asked for it and click **Next** then **Finish** to complete the process.

You have to repeat this procedure to add all your other computers on your home network to the HomeGroup. Quite a tedious operation, but is doesn't take long and in the end is well worth the trouble.

Accessing HomeGroup Computers

Once the HomeGroup is created and all your home computers are joined, accessing their shared libraries is very easy. Just open up Windows Explorer and click on

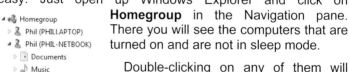

Fig. 10.11

Homegroup in the Navigation pane. There you will see the computers that are turned on and are not in sleep mode.

Double-clicking on any of them will open up all their libraries, as shown for us in Fig. 10.11. Clicking on a library will open up all the folders and files in it. Very quick, easy and useful.

Leaving a HomeGroup

A Windows 7 computer can only be joined to one HomeGroup at a time. You must leave one before joining another, maybe due to a change of the HomeGroup password. To do this go to the HomeGroup window from the Control panel and click the **Leave the homegroup** link, as shown in Fig. 10.9.

Sharing Controls

You can control how you share libraries, folders, drives and even individual files in your HomeGroup and networks. You can set who can share and what rights they have while doing it. This is most easily done with the Sharing Wizard which is enabled by default. If you ever need to re-enable it, start a Windows Explorer window and use the **Organize**, **Folder and search options** command to open the **Folder Options** box. In the View tab check that the **Use Sharing Wizard** option is ticked as in Fig. 10.12 and click **OK**.

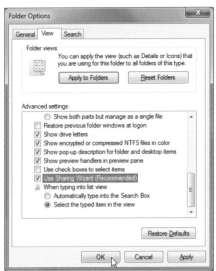

Fig. 10.12 Setting Folder Options

To set sharing options, open an Explorer window, navigate to and select the library, folder, or files that you want to share and either, right-click on the selection and select **Share with**, or click the **Share with** button. Both give four menu options as shown in Fig. 10.13 below. Selecting:

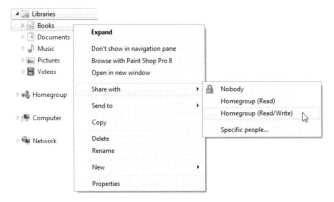

Fig. 10.13 Selecting Sharing Options

Nobody – Prevents the sharing of the selected items. This can be useful if you want to keep some files private. You can quickly filter out what you don't want shared in a library or folder.

Homegroup (Read) – Allows the sharing of the selected items over your HomeGroup but with read only permissions. Other computers in the HomeGroup will be able to view, or read them, but not modify them in any way.

Homegroup (Read/Write) – Allows the sharing of the selected items over your HomeGroup with full permissions to read and make changes to all the files in the selection.

Specific people – Opens the File sharing Wizard and allows you to share the selected items with the HomeGroup and with users on any network you are connected to.

If you select any of the first three options, you may have to confirm what you want, but the sharing then takes place straight away. With the **Specific people** option you have to select or add people you want to share with as in Fig. 10.14.

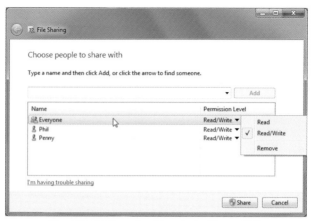

Fig. 10.14 Choosing People to Share With

To choose people on your network to share with click the down-arrow in the top empty box, select them from the list and click the **Add** button. To set their permission level just click them in the **Name** list and select from the opened box, as shown in Fig. 10.14. This is the method you use to give sharing rights to people outside your HomeGroup.

Sharing a Drive

In Windows 7 you can't share system folders or an entire drive (such as an internal or external hard disc) using the **Share with** menu. It's probably not a good idea to share Windows system folders or the drive with Windows installed on it, but can be very useful to share other drives containing data or media. To do this, you use Advanced sharing.

Fig. 10.15 The Advanced Sharing Option

To use Advanced sharing select the drive in the Navigation pane of an Explorer window, click the **Share with** button, and then click **Advanced sharing**, as in Fig. 10.15.

Fig. 10.16 Accessing Advanced Sharing

This opens the **Properties** dialogue box for the drive with the Sharing tab open as shown in Fig. 10.16. In our case the J: external USB drive is shown as **Not shared**. To change this click the **Advanced Sharing** button and give the administrator password or confirmation if either is required, to open the Advanced Sharing box (Fig. 10.17).

Fig. 10.17 The Advanced Sharing Box

Ticking the check box next to **Share this folder** will allow network access to the drive. To control the type of access, or specify users, click on **Permissions** to open the box shown in Fig. 10.18 below.

Fig. 10.18 A Permissions Dialogue Box

Click **Add** or **Remove** to add or remove users or groups and give access permissions to them by clicking the check boxes in the **Permissions for**.. section. If you need help here you can click the **Learn about access control and permissions** link.

To finish click **OK** twice to get back to the drive Properties box (Fig. 10.16). You should see that the drive is now Shared, as shown for us below.

Fig. 10.19 Our External Drive Now Shared

When you've finished, click **OK** again and the drive should now be accessible from every person or computer on your network that you selected. Of course it needs to be switched on!

Sharing Printers

We saw earlier that all the members of a HomeGroup can share the printers in the group. You can also share printers on your network, even if they are not in a HomeGroup, so everyone in your household can connect as long as the printers and PCs are switched on.

To set up this sharing in Windows 7, open the **Devices and Printers** window from the **Start** Menu, right-click on your printer, select **Printer properties** from the context menu and click the Sharing tab in the box that opens (Fig. 10.20). Select the **Share this printer** check box. If it is greyed out you may have to click the 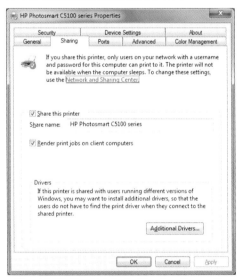 button.

Fig. 10.20 Our Printer's Sharing Properties

Press **OK** to approve the options and close the Properties box.

Before you can use a shared printer from your Windows 7 PC, whether the printer is connected to a Windows 7, Vista, or XP computer, you have to add it to your list of available printers.

To do this, open the **Devices and Printers** window again from the **Start** menu, and click the **Add a printer** button. Select the option to **Add a network, wireless or Bluetooth printer**, and pick your printer from the list.

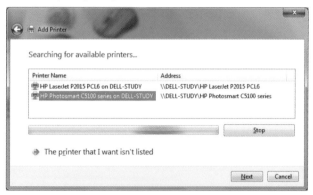

Fig. 10.21 Available Networked Printers

Click **Next**, and wait for the printer driver to be located and loaded. When this is done you can then print a test page to make sure everything works.

Now any computer on the network can select the printer and use it just as if it were directly connected. To illustrate this Fig. 10.22 below shows part of the **Devices and Printers** window from our networked laptop.

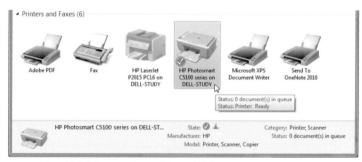

Fig. 10.22 Accessing a Shared Printer over the Network

Network Sharing Settings

You can manually control your network settings from the **Network and Sharing Center** by clicking the **Change advanced sharing settings** link. Please read these below.

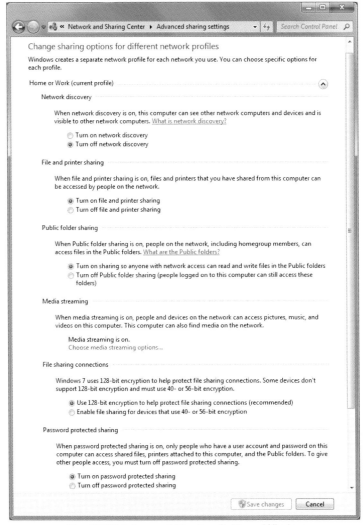

Fig. 10.23 Advanced Sharing Settings Window

As can be seen from Fig. 10.23 the network sharing settings are not very complicated. For home or work networks, it's best to turn on only the features you actually use. For public networks turn everything off to avoid your files and folders being accessed by strangers!

Using the Network

Once all the sharing and permissions have been sorted out you can access the other computers and printers in your network from the usual Explorer window. As shown in Fig. 10.24 they are listed in the **Network** item on the Navigation Pane.

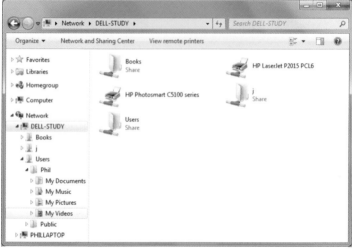

Fig. 10.24 Network as Seen from Our Laptop

Our example above shows how we can access our desktop PC, an external hard disc and two printers in the study, from a networked laptop. We can open and move files between them and even open and stream music and videos. In other words we can start a video located on the desktop and have it play on the laptop. These features are well worth the effort involved.

Mixed PC Wireless Networks

If you have a mix of Windows 7, Vista, and XP, computers and want to set up a simple wireless home network the following notes may be helpful. On each PC do the following:

With Windows XP computers, use the **Start**, **Connect To**, **Show All Connections** menu commands. Select the **Wireless Network Connection** by right-clicking it and selecting **Properties**. Under the General tab, in the main window, you should see **This connection uses the following items**. Scroll down to make sure that **Internet Protocol (TCP/IP)** is in the list. If not, click the **Install** button and then **Protocol**. Highlight **Internet Protocol TCP/IP** in the list and click **OK** to add it. If **Microsoft TCP/IP version 6** is in the list you should add that as well.

Back in the Properties dialogue box, select **Internet Protocol (TCP/IP)** in the list and click the **Properties** button. Check both **Obtain an IP address automatically** and **Obtain DNS server address automatically**, and click **OK** to close the box. Then restart your PC. When it restarts, connect to the network, and you should be able to browse the Internet.

With Vista computers use the **Start**, **Control Panel**, **Network and Sharing Center**, **Manage Network Connections** command sequence. Right-click on **Wireless Network Connection** and proceed as above for Windows XP.

With Windows 7 computers use the **Start**, **Control Panel**, **Network and Sharing Center**, **Change adapter settings**, **Wireless Network Connections** command sequence. Right-click and select **Properties**, and proceed as in Vista and Windows XP. You may have both **TCP/IPv6** and **TCP/IPv4** to select.

Hopefully, at this point, all the computers will be able to connect to the router and access the Internet.

All the computers on the network must each have unique names and must all belong to the same **workgroup**. Windows by default gives workgroups the name **WORKGROUP**. To 'clear the air' at this stage it is a good idea to use a different unique name.

To change the computer name and group name in Windows XP, right-click **My Computer** and select **Properties**. In the Computer Name tab, click the **Change** button. Enter a unique computer name, if the computer does not already have one, and then enter your **new** workgroup name. When you click **OK**, Windows will welcome you to the group and advise you to restart the computer.

To change the computer name and workgroup name in Vista and Windows 7, right-click **Computer** and select **Properties**. Find **Computer name** in the dialogue box and at far right, click **Change settings**. In the **System Properties** box in the **Computer Name** tab, click the **Change** button. Enter your unique computer name, enter the **new** workgroup name you used previously, and leave **Domain** blank. Click **OK**, and Windows will welcome you to the group and ask for a restart.

At this point, all the computers are in the same workgroup and should recognise each other. When switched on they should appear in the **Network** section of the Navigation Pane (Fig. 10.24) of the computer you are using. Each should be able to connect to the router and surf the Internet. Each will be able to access shared and public folders on other devices on the network. If not you will have to sort the sharing properties out as described earlier.

****

Hopefully this brief introduction to networking with Windows 7 will get you up and running. Don't forget that when you make changes to network settings you often have to restart the computer before they become fully effective. Good luck.

11

Looking After Your PC

Windows 7 comes equipped with a full range of utilities for you to easily maintain your PC's health and well being. You can access most of these tools by selecting **System Tools** from the **Start**, **All Programs**, **Accessories** menu, which opens the group of options shown here in Fig. 11.1.

Fig. 11.1 System Tools

Quite an impressive list, but of all the available tools, **System Information** is the easiest to take a first look at – it displays such things as your Operating System, System Summary, Hardware Resources, etc. As each one of these is bound to be different for different PCs, we leave it to you to examine the information for your own system.

Problem Prevention

Windows 7 has strong protection against System corruption:

- System Protection
- Automatic Update
- System Restore

These will be discussed shortly, but now might be a good time to copy your most important data to a DVD or external hard drive, as discussed in Chapter 4. After all, hard discs do 'crash' and your PC could be stolen, or lost in a fire, or flood. Any of these events would cause a serious data loss, so it's a good idea to have copies stored away safely.

System Protection

Windows applications sometimes can, and do, overwrite important **System** files. However, Windows 7 protects your **System** files by automatically saving them at regular intervals, as well as previous versions of files you modify. You can use System Restore to replace the files.

Automatic Update

Fig. 11.2 Windows Update

Windows can automatically update any **System** files as they become available from Microsoft's Web site. To make sure this happens, click the **Start** button 🌐, **All Programs**, and select the **Windows Update** menu option, shown here in Fig. 11.2, and you will be connected to Microsoft's Web site.

Click the **Check for updates** link on the left panel in Fig. 11.3, to get a list of updates for your system. If critical updates are available, these are automatically installed, provided this option was selected (see **Change settings** below). Non-critical updates can be viewed before selecting the ones you might want to install. There is no point downloading updates that have no relevance to you!

The **Change settings** link (second on the list of links on the left panel of Fig. 11.3) displays a window in which you can choose to **Install updates automatically**, as recommended by Microsoft. This should guarantee you are always up to date, which is important to make sure that as possible security issues are found and corrected by Microsoft they are installed on your system straight away.

Fig. 11.3 Checking for Windows Updates

System Restore

 System Restore automatically backs up registry and system files whenever you install new software or drivers, and enables you to restore your computer to an earlier state without losing any of your data files (such as e-mail messages, documents, or photos). You would typically use System Restore if your computer starts misbehaving after an update or a new software installation. Restoring your PC to an earlier restore point may well resolve the problem. Do note, however, that software (programs) installed since the restore point was made will be removed from your PC, **but not data**.

Every time you start to install a new program, System Restore takes a snapshot of your system prior to starting the new installation.

To examine the utility, click the **Start** button 🔵, type **restore** in the search field, and select 🔳 System Restore from the resulting list. You can also use the **Start, All Programs, Accessories, System Tools** menu command and select **System Restore**. Both methods open the first (explanatory) screen of a three-screen **System Restore** utility, as shown in Fig. 11.4 on the next page.

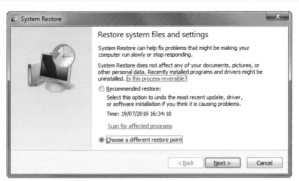

Fig. 11.4 The System Restore Opening Window

Clicking the **Next** button opens the second **System Restore** screen shown in Fig. 11.5 below.

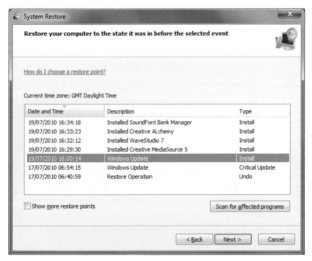

Fig. 11.5 A Recently Available System Restore Point

You may well have more System Restore Points when you try this. Selecting a restore point from the list and clicking **Next** opens the final **System Restore** screen. Once you confirm that this is what you want to do, the restore process starts. Until this process finishes, you should not switch off your computer, or you might end up in real trouble.

To create a new restore point, click the **Start** button 🔵, type **create restore point** in the search field, and select 🖼 Create a restore point from the resulting list. This opens the multi-tab **System Properties** dialogue box, shown in Fig. 11.6 below, with the **System Protection** tab selected.

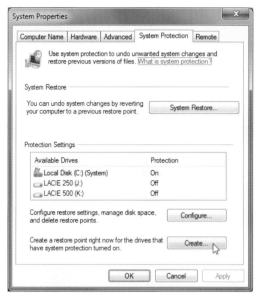

Fig. 11.6 Setting a New System Restore Point

Our two external hard drives above only contain data, not system files, so were not selected by the system. To create a

Fig. 11.7 Creating a Restore Point

System Restore Point, click the **Create** button which displays the box shown in Fig. 11.7.

Next, type a suitable description to identify your restore point, and

click the **Create** button. Windows will notify you of the success or otherwise of the operation.

The System and Security Center

To examine the other options in the Windows **System and Security** center, click the **Start** button ⚫, **Control Panel**, choose to **View by: Category**, and click the **System and Security** icon, shown here, to display the window in Fig. 11.8 below.

Fig. 11.8 The Windows System and Security Center Window

Windows Firewall

For your PC to be secure, make sure that the Windows Firewall is switched on. Clicking the **Check firewall status** link, displays the screen shown in Fig. 11.9 on the next page.

A **Firewall** is a software security system that sits between your computer and the outside world and is used to set restrictions on what information is passed to and from the Internet. In other words it protects you from uninvited access.

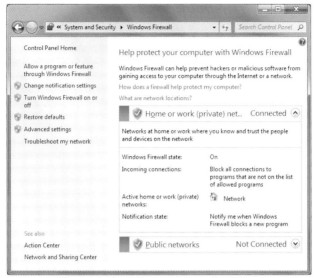

Fig. 11.9 The Windows Firewall Window

If your firewall is turned off, or you do not have up-to-date virus protection, the **Action Center** will flag an error by placing the icon 📳 in the notification area of the Taskbar.

Action Center

The Action Center, new to Windows 7, looks after message alerts from key Windows security and maintenance features.

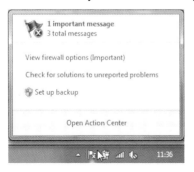

Fig. 11.10 A Pop-up Alert Box

As we saw above, when Windows 7 requires your attention, the Action Center icon appears in the Taskbar. Clicking this icon opens a pop-up box which lists the problems and gives suggested fixes for them. You can click a solution to (hopefully) solve a problem.

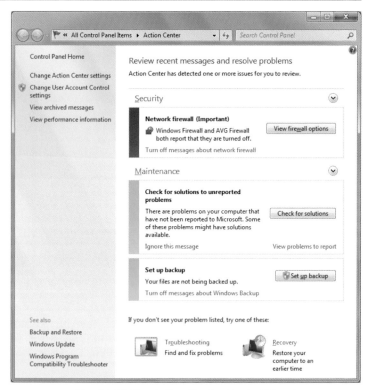

Fig. 11.11 The Action Center Control Panel

Or you can open the Action Center itself (Fig. 11.11) to fine-tune your choices by clicking the **Open Action Center** link. Another way to open the Action Center is by clicking the **Start** button typing **action** and selecting the **Action Center** option from the search result list.

Important items are labelled in red, to indicate that they are significant and should be addressed straight away. In our example above there was no Firewall open, but just clicking the **View firewall options** button let us cure the problem instantly. Yellow items are suggested tasks, such as recommended maintenance tasks, that you should consider doing when you have time.

Power Options

Power Options
Require a password when the computer wakes
Change when the computer sleeps
Change what the power buttons do

This is another tool in the Windows **System and Security** center which gives you control of the power settings of battery powered laptop or netbook computers. Most of these are critical for balancing performance with power usage so that you can maximise the life of each battery charge (see page 200 for more on this).

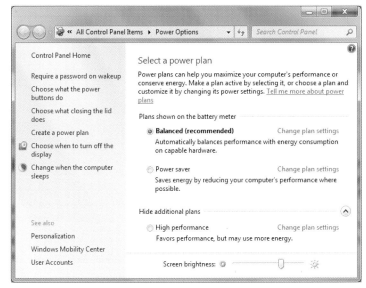

Fig. 11.12 The Power Options Window

Windows Anytime Upgrade

All the versions of Windows 7 (see page 2) are actually included when you install the operating system on your computer. Which version you get to use depends on the product key (page 7) you enter during the installation procedure. At any time in the future you can go online from the **Anytime Upgrade** window and pay for an upgrade to a higher version – maybe Standard to Home Premium. After your purchase Windows 7 will upgrade automatically.

Disk Cleanup

Disk Cleanup locates and removes unnecessary files on your computer and frees up space on your hard drive(s). To start it, click the **Start** button ⬤, type **cleanup** in the search field, and click

Disk Cleanup. Select the drive you want to clean up, as in Fig. 11.13 and click **OK**. **Disk Cleanup** then scans the drive, and lists temporary files, Internet cache files, and other files that you can safely delete, as shown in Fig. 11.14.

Fig. 11.13 Selecting Drive

Fig. 11.14 Files Found that can be Cleaned Up

As you can see, on our setup, we could free some disc space by deleting all the files selected (the longer you use your PC the larger the files that could be deleted), and even more by deleting the **Hibernation File Cleaner** as well, but see the next page first.

Please **do not proceed** with the latter deletion, though, until you highlight its entry and read the displayed small print, or you may have some regrets later, especially if you are using a laptop. If you delete the Hibernation Files, by ticking the check box alongside the **Hibernation File Cleaner** entry, your PC will lose the ability to **Hibernate**, and getting it back can be a bit complicated.

If you don't use hibernation there is no problem. Clicking the **OK** button, starts the cleaning process and removes all the 'unnecessary' files you selected.

Defragmenting your Hard Discs

The **Disk Defragmenter** is also in the **Administrative Tools** section of the **System and Security Center**. It optimises your hard discs by rearranging their data to eliminate unused spaces, which speeds up access by all of Windows operations. By default **Disk Defragmenter** is set to run automatically in Windows 7, but you can also analyse and defragment your discs and drives manually. These days you don't even need to close running applications before starting **Disk Defragmenter**.

You can also start the process by clicking the **Start** button, typing **defrag** in the search field, and selecting ⏏ <u>Disk Defragmenter</u> from the resulting list. Select the disc you want to defragment, and click the **Analyze disk** button to see if the disc needs to be defragmented.

If the percentage of fragmentation on the disc is high, you should click the **Defragment disk** button and start the process. You can defragment a drive in the background by minimising the window to the **Taskbar** and carry on with your work as normal.

Backing up your Data

 Anyone can lose files by: accidentally deleting or replacing them, a virus attack, or a software or hardware failure, such as a complete hard disc failure. With Windows, you can use **System Restore** to recover your system files, you can reinstall your programs, but what about your precious data files? To protect these, you should regularly create backups, or sets of copies of your data files, stored in a different location.

Too many people don't think about backing up their data until it has already been lost! Please don't let this happen to you. Windows 7 makes backing up easy, and has a range of features to seamlessly protect your data and system setup.

Unlike Vista all the versions of Windows 7 allow you to either back up your data files or make a complete backup of the drives required for Windows (or others) by creating a system image that can be used later to restore a broken PC.

Data Backup

Windows 7 supports both automatic and manual data backup options, enabling you to choose which files to back up and when. You can then restore your backups at any time to recover previous versions of documents, or to replace a file you may have accidentally deleted.

System Image

In Windows 7 the System Image Backup feature creates a system image or snapshot containing the entire contents of the drives required for Windows 7 to run (usually the C: drive). If you need to recover your PC, you can simply restore the system image and get right back to work. Unfortunately you can't save an automatically generated system image on a flash drive, only on a fixed hard drive. To include other drives in a system image, or store it on a flash drive or DVDs, you have to manually carry out the backup.

Windows 7 Professional and Ultimate versions also support automated network-based backups, but we have not looked at that here.

The Backup and Restore Center

This is where you carry out your PC backup. However, before you start, it should be obvious that making a complete PC backup requires you to have some sort of an external hard drive or flash disc that plugs into a USB port, that is at least the same size as the internal drive. These do not cost a lot these days, but believe us money spent here is well worth it. If you have one, plug it in now.

You can open the **Backup and Restore** center from the **Control Panel** but it is easier to click the **Start** button⬤, type **backup** in the search field, and select 📁 Backup and Restore from the resulting list. This opens the window shown in Fig. 11.15.

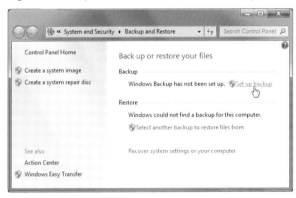

Fig. 11.15 The Backup and Restore Center

As you can see, the first time you initiate this procedure, you are required to configure **backup**, by clicking the **Set up**

Fig. 11.16 Configuring Backup

backup link pointed to above. This opens the window shown in Fig. 11.16 asking you to wait while Windows has a look at your system to see whether you have a suitable drive on which to make the backup.

The Set up backup window, shown in Fig. 11.17 below, opens next in which you are prompted to select the location to save your backup.

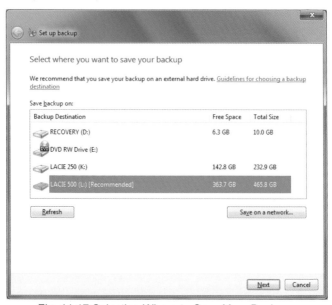

Fig. 11.17 Selecting Where to Save Your Backup

In this case, the L: drive, recommended for the backup, was one of two external USB drives. In this computer drive D: was a partition on the C: drive which holds all the system recovery data files. All of our data folders and files are in folders and Libraries on the C: drive itself. Yours is probably very much the same.

Make your selection and click the **Next** button which opens the window shown in Fig. 11.18 on the next page. Here you are asked to decide what you want to do. The recommended choice will make a complete backup of your PC, while the second choice allows you to specify what you want to back up and whether to include an image of your system or not.

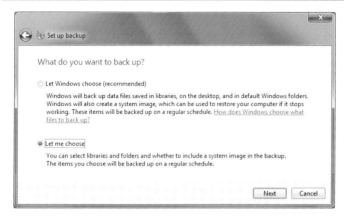

Fig. 11.18 Choosing an Option for the Backup

Selecting the first option is almost automatic. The second choice (**Let me choose**), displays the window in Fig. 11.19 below in which we have selected all our Libraries, some additional data folders in the folders tree, but not to **Include a system image of drive C:**.

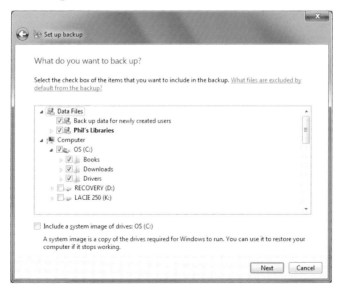

Fig. 11.19 Selecting What to Include in the Backup

The next window (Fig. 11.20) gives a summary of what you have chosen to back up and when future backups will be made. If you click the **Change schedule** link, you can set how often you want backups to be automatically carried out, these can be daily, weekly or monthly. The first time you do this, Windows carries out a full backup of your data files, later scheduled backups will only include new, or modified, files. Choose the settings you want and click the **Save settings and run backup** button.

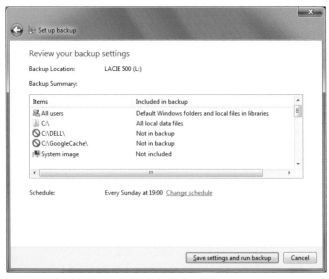

Fig. 11.20 Setting the Schedule for Creating Backups

The backup process then starts, as shown in Fig. 11.21 on the next page. This can take some time, depending on your system and on how much data is being backed up. Our first full backup took several hours, but subsequent ones usually take a lot less time. This is no problem though, as you can carry on working during the process.

To see how the backup process is going, click the **View Details** button. This opens an additional window with a progress bar and a **Stop backup** button you can click to end the process at any time.

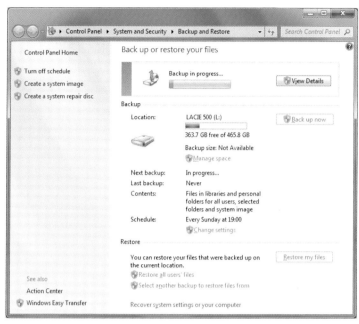

Fig. 11.21 The Backup and Restore Control Panel

Subsequent Backups

Once you create the initial backup, you really never have to think about backing up your files again since Windows will regularly do this for you according to the schedule you set.

 When you create a backup, a special backup folder is placed on the destination drive. Double-clicking its icon (shown here), opens the window shown in Fig. 11.22. From here you can restore your files, or manage the space used by your backups. You can, for instance, delete older backups to save disc space.

Fig. 11.22 Configuring Backup

Restoring from Backups

Restoring files and folders from your backups is very easy. You do it from the **Backup and Restore** center (see page 183), shown in Fig. 11.23 below.

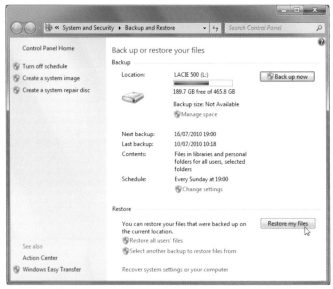

Fig. 11.23 The Backup and Restore Center

Clicking the **Restore my files** button, starts the procedure for restoring specific files and folders from the last backup.

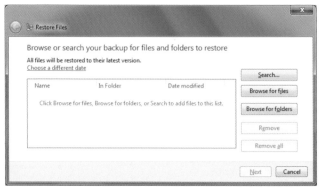

Fig. 11.24 The Restore Files Screen

You can select whether you want to restore files from the latest or an older backup, browse for files or folders, or search for a specific file or folder, before clicking the **Next** button to continue.

Fig. 11.25 Selecting a Data File to Restore

Select the files or folders you want to restore, then click the **Add files** button to display the window in Fig. 11.26.

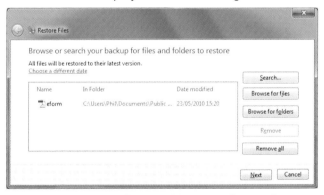

Fig. 11.26 The Selected Files to be Restored

Clicking the **Next** button, opens the window shown in Fig. 11.27 on the next page in which you are asked where you want to restore the selected file(s).

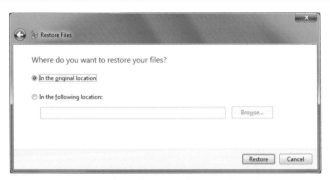

Fig. 11.27 Specifying the Restore Location

You would normally pick to restore your selection to their original location, unless you want them somewhere else of course. Finally click the **Restore** button which displays the window in Fig. 11.28.

Fig. 11.28 The Copy File Window

To restore everything from the latest backup, start the **Backup and restore** center, click the **Restore my files** button (see Fig. 11.23), then click the **Browse for folders** button (see Fig. 11.24) and finally click the actual backup folder on the left on the screen of Fig. 11.29 and select in turn each sub-folder (in our case Backup of C: and Backup of K:) and press the **Add folder** button after each selection. In this way all the files on drives C: and K: will be restored.

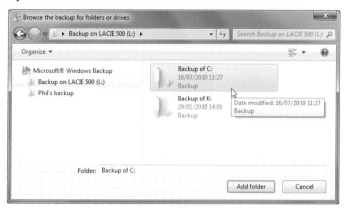

Fig. 11.29 Restoring Everything from a Backup

We are very impressed with Windows 7's backup and restore facilities. They are easy to use, and once you have set a procedure in motion you can forget it, safe in the knowledge that your data files are being regularly protected. Don't forget to do a complete backup every few months though!

If you have enough room on your external storage drive, backing up an image of your PC's drive (by either selecting the **Include a system image** option in Fig. 11.19, or using the **Create a system image** option in the **Backup and Restore** center), is a good idea.

A system image is a copy of the drive required for Windows to run, and can be used to restore your computer if the hard drive breaks down. However, you cannot restore individual files from a system image backup, only the full image. A system image is a particularly good idea just after you have installed Windows 7 and have all your drivers and working programs set up and running. Your PC will be uncluttered and will be running at its fastest then. If disaster strikes that is a good place to rapidly restore your system to. All you will have to do then is download updates and restore your data files.

Windows Defender

Windows Defender is free anti-spyware software included with Windows 7. It helps protect your computer against spyware and other potentially dangerous software being installed on your computer when you are connected to the Internet. It offers two ways to help keep infections at bay.

In real-time, it alerts you when spyware attempts to install itself, to run on your computer, or to change Windows settings.

You can also scan for spyware that might be installed on your computer and automatically remove problems.

Fig. 11.30 Notification Window

To open Windows Defender **click** the **Start** button, type **Defender**, and select Windows Defender from the list. If it is not turned on you may get a message asking you to **click here to turn it on**.

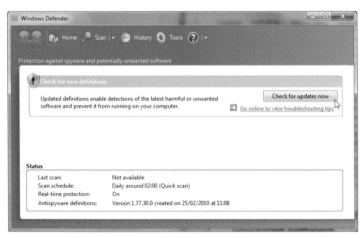

Fig. 11.31 Checking for Definitions Updates

The first time it is opened you will get a window like ours in Fig. 11.31 asking you to **Check for new definitions**. With Windows Defender, it is very important to have up-to-date 'definitions', or files listing potential software threats. Once it is switched on the program will work with Windows Update to automatically install new definitions and keep them up to date.

With Windows Defender you can run two types of scan of your computer:

Quick scan checks the most likely places on your hard disc that spyware will be located. This is the default type and is actioned when you click **Scan**.

Full scan checks all your files and all currently running programs, but will seriously slow down your computer while it is taking place. To start this procedure click the arrow next to the **Scan** button, and select **Full scan**.

Microsoft recommends that you schedule a daily quick scan and to only run a full scan if you think that your computer is infected.

The real-time spyware protection alerts you when spyware or other potentially unwanted software tries to install itself, or run, on your PC. You can then choose one of several actions:

Quarantine moves it to a safe location on your computer, and prevents it from running, unless you choose to restore it.

Remove permanently deletes the software from your computer.

Allow adds the software to the Defender allowed list and lets it run on your computer. You should only use this if you trust the software and the software publisher.

For more in-depth information we suggest you look at Windows Defender **Help** accessed by clicking the ⑦ button.

User Account Control

UAC, or User Account Control, is a very important Windows 7 security feature which helps to prevent unauthorised changes to your computer by programs, viruses or other users through a network.

When an application (or program) tries to make system changes such as: the installation of new software, modifications of system files and folders, or modifications which affect other users, UAC prompts you to ask for permission, as in Fig. 11.32.

Fig. 11.32 A User Account Control Prompt

If you click **No** the change is not performed. If you click **Yes** you give the application administrative permissions to make system changes during the current session (see page 113).

The easiest way to open User Account Control is to click the **Start** button, type **uac** in the Search box and select the ⟨Change User Account Control settings⟩ option. Alternatively, you can find it with the **Control Panel**, **System and Security**, **Action Center**, **Change User Account Control settings** command sequence (Fig. 11.8).

The UAC window that opens has a slider as shown in Fig. 11.33 on the facing page. You can drag this slider to change your UAC settings. By default, as shown, it is set to notify you only when programs try to make changes to your computer. This is the best setting to use. It gives good protection and only bothers you when you try to open an old program, or when something dangerous can happen.

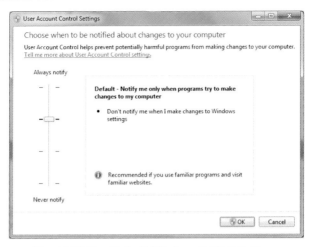

Fig. 11.33 The Default Windows 7 UAC Settings

The four UAC levels to choose from are:

1. Always notify – The most secure setting but very annoying. You are always notified before any changes are made. The UAC prompt opens and your Desktop background is dimmed. You cannot use your computer until you choose **Yes** or **No**. We don't recommend this setting!

2. Notify me only when programs try to make changes to my computer – The default level which only prompts before programs make changes to your computer that require administrative permissions. This level is less annoying as it doesn't stop you making changes to the system, but only shows prompts if an application wants to make changes. The Desktop is still dimmed and you must choose **Yes** or **No** before you can do anything else on your computer. This is the setting we use.

3. Notify me only when programs try to make changes to my computer (do not dim my desktop) – Identical to 2 above except that the Desktop is not dimmed. This level is less secure as it is easier for malicious programs to simulate keystrokes or mouse moves which interfere with the UAC prompt.

4. Never notify – UAC is turned off and doesn't offer any protection. We don't recommend this setting, with UAC turned off it is much easier for rogue programs to infect your computer and even take control of it.

With Windows Vista, UAC was a real headache for most users. This is no longer the case with Windows 7, as you have more control over the settings, which can provide a good balance between security and usability.

Please don't turn off UAC or you will regret it one day!

12

Mobility and Accessibility

Mobility

By mobility we are referring here to computer mobility, not yours! One of the nice things about using Windows 7 on a **mobile** notebook or netbook PC is that the most important configuration options are consolidated into a single utility, the **Windows Mobility Center**. This is where you should go when you want to control how your mobile PC works.

Windows Mobility Center

To launch the Mobility Center, open the **Start** menu and select **All Programs**, **Accessories**, **Windows Mobility Center**. An easier way is to click the **Start** button, type **mobility** in the Search box and select Windows Mobility Center. Either method opens a window like ours in Fig. 12.1.

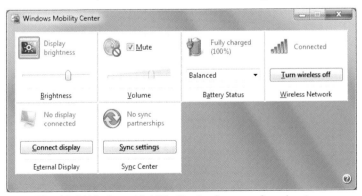

Fig. 12.1 Windows Mobility Center for one of our Laptops

The Mobility Center, as shown in Fig. 12.1, includes panels for the most common laptop settings.

Brightness

A slider temporarily adjusts the display brightness. If you hover the mouse over the display icon it turns into a button which opens the **Power Options** window, where you can change the brightness level on your current power plan.

Volume

Adjusts the volume level of your computer's sound and lets you mute it. Click the speaker graphic and Windows opens the **Sound** dialogue box, which you can use to adjust all the audio settings on your laptop.

Battery Status

Displays the current charge status of your computer's battery and lets you change the power plan. Clicking the battery graphic, opens the **Power Options** window (Fig. 12.4), where you can edit the power plans and create your own custom power plans, as discussed in the next section.

Wireless Network

Shows your current wireless status and lets you turn the wireless adaptor on or off. Clicking the **Change wireless settings** button opens the panel (Fig. 10.3) listing the available wireless networks in the area. From this you can connect to an available network or open the **Network and Sharing Center**.

External Display

Lets you connect your laptop to an external monitor or projector. Clicking the [Connect display] button opens the window shown in Fig. 12.2 on the facing page.

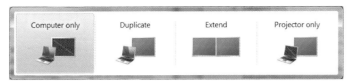

Fig. 12.2 Controlling External Display Devices

Where, **Computer Only** leaves any external display blank. **Duplicate** shows the same display on the internal and external monitors. **Extend** lets you create a large desktop stretching between the internal and external displays, and **Projector Only** sends your computer signal to the external display only. This is good for giving a presentation.

Clicking the display graphic button opens the **Screen Resolution** window, which you can use to change the resolution and orientation (landscape or portrait) of both your internal and external displays.

Sync Center

Lets you check the results of your recent synchronisation activity if you've set up your computer to sync files with a network server. Unfortunately this does not yet work with other connected drives or gadgets.

All in all this is a very useful facility for mobile users. Depending on your system, the Mobility Center may show more panels (such as Screen Rotation for a Tablet PC or Presentation Settings). Also some notebook manufacturers add their own panels.

Just in case you wondered, the Mobility Center by default, is only available on laptops, netbooks, and tablet PCs. It is not available on desktop computers unless it is enabled.

Power Plans

If you are anything like us when using a laptop away from the mains you will always be worrying about how much power you are using. Even the best batteries seem to run low far too early!!

As well as the Battery Status tile in the Mobility Center, the battery meter in the Notification Area of the Taskbar (page 16) shows you what state your laptop battery is in. If you hover over it, the % charge appears. If you click it, a pop-up like that in Fig. 12.3 opens showing what power plan is active.

Fig. 12.3

The Windows 7 **Power Plans** cater for three main power designs that can help you save energy, maximise system performance, or achieve a balance between the two.

To see the default power plans, click **More power options** in the above pop-up to open the Power Options window shown in Fig. 12.4. You can also open Power Options from the Battery Status tile in the Mobility Center, or by clicking the **Start** button, and typing **power options** in the search box, or by just selecting it in the Control Panel.

The three default **Power Plans** are:

Balanced – Giving good performance when it is needed, but saving power during periods of inactivity.

Power saver – Saves power by reducing screen brightness and system performance. This can be useful if you are ever 'caught out'.

High performance – Giving maximum brightness and performance, but using far more power, making it rather unhelpful to mobile users unless they are plugged in to the mains. This doesn't appear on the battery meter by default, you have to select it from the Power Options window by clicking **Show additional plans**, and then **High performance**.

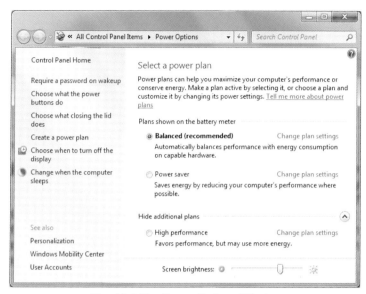

Fig. 12.4 The Power Options Window

Which plan to use? For most people much of the time the default **Balanced** plan is a good compromise between battery life and performance. Many people will never leave it.

When you are away from home and operating on batteries the **Power saver** plan will probably give you a few more minutes of battery life.

You should only really use the **High performance** plan when you are connected to mains power and have a full battery charge.

These three power plans should meet your needs most of the time, but if you want to build your own, then you can use one of the default power plans as a starting point. All of them can be adapted by clicking on their **Change plan settings** link in the Power Options window. The main settings in the **Edit Plan Settings** windows that open are when to **Turn off the display**, and when to **Put the computer to sleep**. But the **Change advanced power settings** link gives you almost absolute control over everything, as shown in Fig. 12.5.

Fig. 12.5 Changing Advanced Power Settings

Conserving Battery Power

There are several things you can do when your mobile computer is running low away from a source of power.

- Use the **Power saver** power plan.

- Reduce display brightness. This uses more power than any other part of a computer. Most laptops have a dedicated key to change the display brightness, or you can adjust brightness from the Mobility Center.

- Shorten the length of time before Windows dims and turns off the display after a period of inactivity.

- Turn off or disconnect devices that you are not actually using. For example many USB devices use power just by being connected. You can save power by disconnecting a USB mouse and using the touch pad instead. Also unplug an external USB flash drive when it's not actually being used.

- Turn off PC cards and integrated wireless devices They all use power so turn them off when they are not needed.

The Ease of Access Center

If you have problems using a standard computer Windows 7 has several features that may be of help.

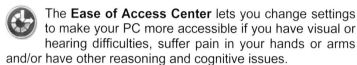 The **Ease of Access Center** lets you change settings to make your PC more accessible if you have visual or hearing difficulties, suffer pain in your hands or arms and/or have other reasoning and cognitive issues.

The easiest way to open the **Ease of Access Center** is the 🪟+U keyboard shortcut. A longer way is the **Control Panel**, **Ease of Access**, **Ease of Access Center** command sequence. Both methods open the window in Fig. 12.6 below.

Fig. 12.6 The Ease of Access Center

The **Ease of Access Center** includes a quick access panel at the top with a highlight rotating through the four most common tools; **Magnifier**, **Narrator**, **On-Screen Keyboard**, and **High Contrast**. A voice, the Narrator, also tells you what option is selected. Pressing the **Spacebar** on a highlighted option will start it for you.

If the Narrator annoys you, click the **Always read this section aloud** box to remove the tick mark from it. While you are doing this, you could also remove the tick mark from the **Always scan this section** box, to stop the focus from rotating between the four entries.

The ♡ **Get recommendations...** link opens a five-stage questionnaire. Depending on your answers to questions about performing routine tasks, such as whether you have difficulty seeing faces or text on TV, hearing conversations, or using a pen or pencil, Windows 7 will provide a recommendation of the accessibility settings and programs that are likely to improve your ability to see, hear and use your computer. This has to be a good place to start.

The **Explore all settings** section at the bottom of the **Ease of Access Center** lets you explore settings options by categories. When selected, these will automatically start each time you log on to the computer. They include:

- Using the computer without a display

- Making the computer easier to see

- Using the computer without a mouse or keyboard

- Changing mouse or keyboard settings

- Using text or visual alternatives for sounds

- Making it easier to focus on tasks.

In the next few pages we will give you an overview of these various options, but we will not discuss any of them in too much detail, as different people have different and specific needs!

The Microsoft Magnifier

To start the Magnifier, click on **Start Magnifier** (words not icon) shown in Fig. 12.6.

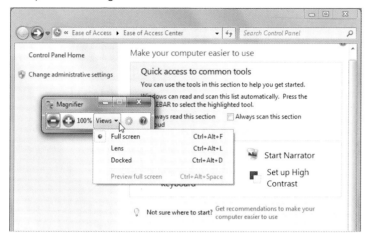

Fig. 12.7 Computer Screen with the Magnifier Active

The new Magnifier window has two views: **Full screen** (the default as shown above), and **Lens**, selected from the **Views** drop-down list shown open in Fig. 12.7. In **Lens** view, wherever you place the mouse pointer the screen is magnified. The Magnifier window allows you to increase ⊕ or decrease ⊖ the magnification, or use the Options icon ⚙ to turn on colour inversion, select tracking options and fine-tune screen fonts.

   If you don't use the Magnifier window for more than a few seconds, it turns into an actual magnifying glass icon, as shown here. Clicking this Magnifier icon again, re-opens the Magnifier window shown in Fig. 12.7.

To close down the Magnifier, click the **Close** button ▬▬ ✕ ▬▬ in the Magnifier window.

This feature takes a while to get used to, but it can be well worthwhile trying it out.

Microsoft Narrator

Narrator is a basic screen reader built into Windows and may be useful for the visually impaired. It reads dialogue boxes and window controls in a number of Windows basic applications, as long as the computer being used has a sound card and speakers or headphones.

To open it, click the **Start Narrator** option in the **Ease of Access Center** (Fig. 12.6). Anna will start speaking in an electronic voice and the Microsoft Narrator window will open, as shown in Fig. 12.8. This is where you can customise and control the **Narrator**.

Fig. 12.8 Microsoft Narrator

If you find this facility useful you will need to play around with the **Main Narrator Settings** until you get it working the best way for you. To close **Narrator** just click the **Exit** button.

The On-Screen Keyboard

To activate the **On-Screen Keyboard** (Fig. 12.9), click the **Start On-Screen Keyboard** option in the **Ease of Access Center** shown earlier in Fig. 12.6.

Fig. 12.9 The On-Screen Keyboard

This excellent new virtual keyboard opens on the screen and allows users with mobility impairments to type data using a mouse pointer, a joystick, or other pointing device. The result is exactly as if you were using the actual keyboard. It has three typing modes selected when the **Options** key is clicked. These are:

Clicking mode – you click the on-screen keys to type text.

Hovering mode – you use a mouse or joystick to point to a key for a predefined period of time, and the selected character is typed automatically.

Scanning mode – the **On-Screen Keyboard** continually scans the keyboard and highlights areas where you can type keyboard characters by pressing a hot key or using a switch-input device.

You can also adjust the settings for your 'physical' keyboard by clicking the ▱ **Make the keyboard easier to use** entry towards the bottom of the **Ease of Access Center** window, and selecting various options on the displayed window.

Turn on Mouse Keys lets you move the mouse pointer by pressing the arrow keys on the keyboard's numeric pad.

Turn on Sticky Keys allows you to press the **Ctrl**, **Alt**, and **Shift**, keys one at a time, instead of all at the same time. This is useful for people who have difficulty pressing two or more keys at a time.

Turn on Toggle Keys makes your PC play a high-pitched sound when the **Caps Lock**, **Scroll Lock**, or **Num Lock** keys are used. The **Turn on Filter Keys** option tells the keyboard to ignore brief or repeated keystrokes.

The Display Options

To make your screen easier to see you can try the **Set up High Contrast** option in Fig. 12.6. This opens a window in which you can set programs to change their colour-specific schemes to a **High Contrast** scheme, change the size of text, set the thickness of the blinking cursor, etc.

The Mouse Options

Clicking the 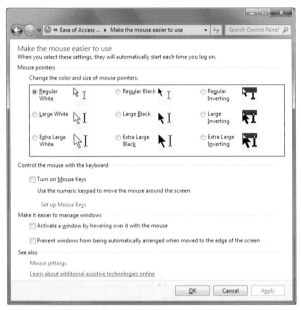 **Make the mouse easier to use** link near the bottom of Fig. 12.6, displays the window below.

Fig. 12.10 Making the Mouse Easier to Use

Here you can change the colour and size of the mouse pointer, and control the mouse pointer's movements with the keys on the numeric keypad.

Clicking the **Set up Mouse Keys** link, displays an additional window in which you can control, amongst other things, the speed at which the mouse pointer moves, and the shortcut key combination you need to activate and deactivate the numeric keypad.

We will leave it to you to explore the other settings on the list in the lower half of the **Ease of Access Center**. It is the only way of finding out what suits you personally. Good luck!

13

Accessories and Games

Like its predecessors Windows 7 comes with some very useful accessory programs. Most of these have been completely revamped for Windows 7 though, and some are good enough to be ranked as 'stand alone' programs.

Don't forget also the programs mentioned in earlier chapters that Microsoft has made available in their Windows Live Essentials free download. When you have downloaded all these you really do have a powerful group of applications at your disposal.

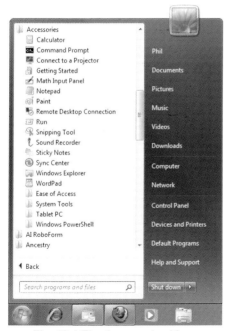

We only have the space here to briefly describe the main accessories and show a few screen downloads, but they all come with quite comprehensive Help and are easy to use.

They are not all included with all the versions of Windows 7, so if you can't find one you probably don't have it!

You can open them from the **Start**, **All Programs** menu in the **Accessories** folder shown here in Fig. 13.1.

Fig. 13.1 The Accessories Menu

Paint

The new Windows 7 version of Paint is a genuinely useful and easy-to-use application for drawing and editing pictures or digital photographs. You can use it to create drawings on a blank drawing area or add to existing pictures. This makes it useful for both youngsters who want to play and professionals who need a quick and lightweight image editor. With this in mind Paint now saves its files in **.PNG** format by default. That is the format all the images in this book were saved in.

To open **Paint**, click the **Start** button 🏵, then click **All Programs**, **Accessories**, and then the   Paint   option.

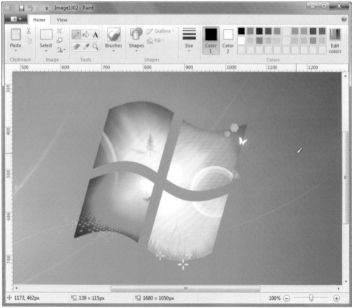

Fig. 13.2 Some of the Default Windows 7 Opening Screen in Paint

As can be seen above the new version of Paint is bang up to date. All the previous menus and toolbars have been replaced with an Office 2010 style Ribbon across the top.

Fig. 13.3 The Opening Help Page on Using Paint

Once you have experimented a little you should find that most of its options are self-explanatory, but to get more on a feature just clicking the **Help** button 🔘, or using the **F1** shortcut, opens a very detailed series of Help articles, the first one of which is shown in Fig. 13.3 above.

The Home tab includes all the brushes and shapes and the tools for image manipulation such as re-sizing, flipping, cropping and changing colours. The View tab has the Zoom tools, as well as Rulers and Gridlines for when you need to do detailed work in Paint. All in all we are impressed and hope you will give it a try.

WordPad

 WordPad is a text-editing program you can use to create and edit documents. Unlike Notepad, WordPad documents can include rich formatting and graphics, and you can link to, or embed objects, like pictures.

WordPad can be used to open and save text documents (**.txt**), rich text files (**.rtf**), Word documents (**.docx**), and OpenDocument Text (**.odt**) documents. Documents in other formats are opened as plain text documents.

To open WordPad, click the **Start** button , then click **All Programs**, **Accessories**, and then the WordPad option.

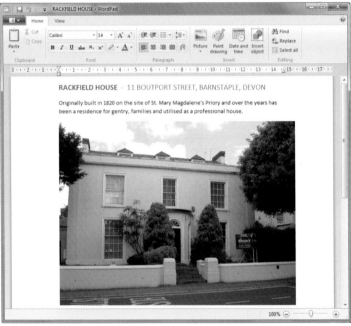

Fig. 13.4 Some of WordPad's New Features

The new ribbon, formatting options like highlighting, bullets, and colours, zoom and picture insertion, makes WordPad a pleasure to use for your basic word-processing.

As with all programs that have a ribbon across the top, (Paint for example) clicking the **Application** button  (or the **Alt+F** keyboard shortcut) opens the application menu where you can do the usual 'File menu' type operations like Open, Save and Print the current document.

Fig. 13.5 The Application Button Menu for WordPad

Once WordPad is open you just get on with typing your document into the working area. All the formatting and layout controls are on the Home tab of the ribbon. To insert a picture click the **Picture** button and select its file. The **Paint drawing** option opens the Paint program for you to create a drawing. The **Zoom** and **Ruler** controls are in the View tab.

Have a look at the Quick Access toolbar on the left of the window Title bar. It has icons for saving and undoing and redoing actions. You can also add more quick actions here.

If necessary, click the **Page setup** option in the Application Button Menu (Fig. 13.5). In the same menu you can then **Print**, **Save**, or **Send in e-mail** before clicking **Exit** to close WordPad. We like this simple to use program.

Notepad

Notepad is a text editor which can be used to read or write short notes, or create and edit script files with the **.txt** extension. It has not noticeably changed with Windows 7. To open Notepad, click the **Start** button 🌀, then click **All Programs**, **Accessories**, and then the ⬜ Notepad option.

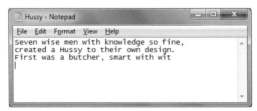

Fig. 13.6 Typing a Text File into Notepad

Although Notepad is not as powerful as WordPad, it has some interesting features, such as the ability to turn on word wrap which places words that will not fit within its page margins on the next line automatically. You can turn word wrap on by selecting the **Format**, **Word Wrap** menu command.

To change the font of a selected text, use the **Format**, **Font** command and use the Font dialogue box. You can change the **Font style** and font **Size** of your text document. However, any changes you make here are reflected in the whole document, as well as all later documents you open in Notepad. You are actually configuring Notepad to the font, font style and font size you would like to use when reading or writing text files, rather than applying these changes to whole or parts of a document.

Notepad supports the usual edit features, such as cut, copy, paste, and delete, in the **Edit** menu. The **Select All** option allows you to highlight a whole document at a stroke so as to copy it onto the Windows **Clipboard**. You can even use Notepad to search and find text, by selecting the **Edit**, **Find** command. Once the text is found, pressing the **F3** key finds the next occurrence. You can also control the **Direction** of the search and use the **Match case** facility.

The New Calculator

With Windows 7, Calculator has received quite a major update and it now works with touch-compatible displays. If you have a suitable touch screen you can actually 'press' the Calculator buttons, but unfortunately we can't. It also now supports several different operating modes.

To open Calculator, click the **Start** button 🔵, then click **All Programs**, **Accessories**, and then the 🔲 Calculator option.

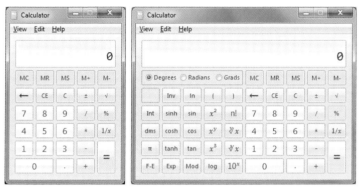

Fig. 13.7 Calculator in Standard (left) and Scientific Modes

Calculator Modes

Standard – The classic Windows Calculator mode (**Alt+1**) similar to that with all Windows versions since Windows 95. This lets you do simple calculations like addition, subtraction, multiplication, and division by clicking the calculator buttons, or typing calculations in using your keyboard.

One change is that it now has an **M-** button (Memory Subtract) to go with the **MC** (Memory Clear), **MR** (Memory Recall), **MS** (Memory Store), and **M+** (Memory Add) buttons.

Scientific – To change to this mode use the **View**, **Scientific** menu command or the **Alt+2** keyboard shortcut. To access inverse functions, click the **Inv** key. In Scientific mode the Calculator is precise to 32 digits and honours operator precedence.

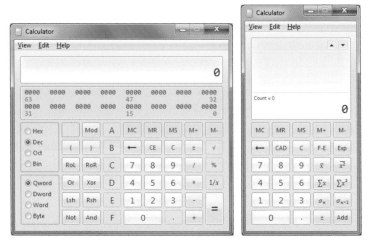

Fig. 13.8 Calculator in Programmer (left) and Statistics Modes

Programmer – To change to this mode use the **View**, **Programmer** menu command or the **Alt+3** shortcut. This mode is new to Windows 7 and provides such things as number format (hexadecimal, decimal, octal, binary) conversions and data type (Byte, Word, Dword, Qword) conversions.

Programmer mode is an integer only mode and is precise up to 64 bits, depending on the word size used. Decimal portions are discarded.

Statistics – To change to this new mode use the **View**, **Statistics** menu command or the **Alt+4** shortcut.

We think Microsoft assumes that if you want to use these last two modes you will already be familiar with the button markings! Some tool tips here would certainly have been helpful. The **Help** menu, or the **F1** shortcut, does give some details of how to use Statistics mode, but not the others.

There are several other Calculator functions on the **View** menu, including the ability to convert values from one unit of measurement to another, to calculate dates and to calculate such things as fuel economy, lease or mortgage payments. Lots to play with here.

Sticky Notes

Do you have trouble remembering things? If so, this accessory lets you plaster electronic Post-It notes all over your Windows 7 desktop. You can even colour code them to help you keep organised and they will stay wherever you put them until they are deleted.

To create a Sticky Note, click the **Start** button, then click **All Programs**, **Accessories**, and then click .

Finish Win 7 book
Proof Noel's book
BBQ on Thursday

Fig. 13.9 Sticky Note Reminders

A new blank note opens on the Desktop, with the cursor at the beginning. You just type the text of the note as we did in Fig. 13.9 above.

To format the note, select the text you want and use the **Ctrl+B** for bold, **Ctrl+I** for italic, and **Ctrl+U** for underlined shortcut keys. Text automatically wraps to a new line, and the height of the note automatically expands when necessary.

When you finish entering text, simply click the Desktop outside the note, or click the **New Note** button ⊞ (**Ctrl+N**) to start a new sticky note.

To delete a note you no longer need, click its **Delete Note** button ☒ (**Ctrl+D**) in the upper-right corner. The first time you do this you are asked to confirm the deletion. If you don't want to see this alert again, select the **Don't Display This Message Again** check box before you click **Yes**.

To change the colour of a note, right-click it and select the colour you want, from Blue, Green, Pink, Purple, White, or Yellow.

Snipping Tool

With this tool you can capture screen shots (snips) of anything on your Desktop. It lets you capture a whole window, a rectangular section, or a freehand outline drawn with your mouse, tablet pen, or your finger if you have a touchscreen. Then you can annotate, save, or e-mail the snipped image.

To open the Snipping Tool, click the **Start** button 🔵, then click **All Programs**, **Accessories**, and click ▢ Snipping Tool ▢.

Fig. 13.10 The Snipping Tool

To capture a snip, click the down-arrow next to the **New** button, select **Free-form Snip**, **Rectangular Snip**, **Window Snip**, or **Full-screen Snip** from the list, and then select the area of your screen that you want to capture.

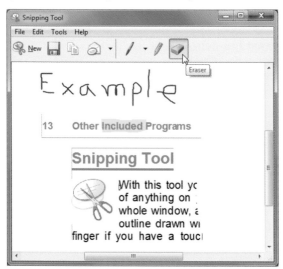

Fig. 13.11 An Annotated Free-form Snip in the Mark-up Window

The new snip opens in the Mark-up window, as shown in Fig. 13.11. In this window you can use the **Pen** , **Highlighter** and **Eraser** tools on the toolbar to annotate it, before saving it , (as an **.HTML**, **.Png**, **.gif**, or **.JPEG** file), copying it to the clipboard , or sending it by e-mail . The **Eraser** only deletes any annotations you have added, not the details of the captured snip.

Games

Windows 7 also comes with a fair selection of games for those moments when you can't think of anything better to do. Not all of them are included in all the versions though.

To open the Games folder for the first time click the **Start** button , type **games** in the search box and then click the Games Explorer entry.

Fig. 13.12 The Games Explorer Window

Access to the games is from the special Games Explorer window as shown here in Fig. 13.12.

To play a game you just double-click on its icon. This window also offers game updates, statistics, news feeds and more. If it doesn't open for you Games might have been turned off in your version of Windows 7. No problem, it's easy to turn on again in the Windows Features box (page 114).

To do this click the **Start** button 🌚, type **features** in the search box and then click the 🔲 Turn Windows features on or off 　 entry.

Fig. 13.13 Turning Games On or Off

Make sure the games you want are ticked and click **OK**.

Customising the Start Menu

A much easier way to access the Games Explorer window in the future is to add it to the main **Start** menu, so it is always just two clicks away. To do this click the **Start** button 🌚 to open the **Start** menu, right-click in an empty section of the coloured bar on the right and select **Properties**. Then click the **Customize** button to open the Customize Start Menu dialogue box shown in Fig. 13.14. This is where you can set up the **Start** menu just how you want. We suggest you have a good look at its options.

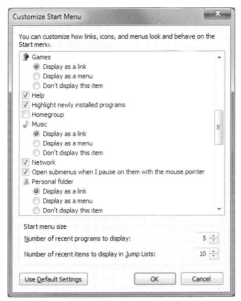

Fig. 13.14 The Customize Start Menu Box

To 'permanently' add Games to the menu, scroll down the list and select the **Games**, **Display as a link** option as shown at the top of Fig. 13.14. Then click on **OK** twice to close the two boxes.

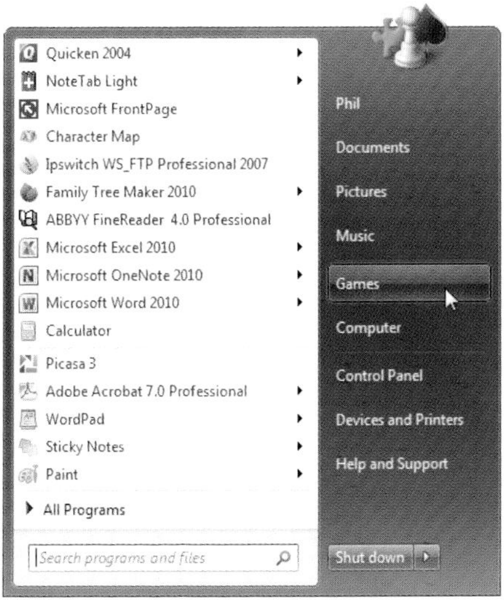

The next time you open the **Start** menu you should see the **Games** option in the list as in Fig. 13.15. You can remove it the same way in the future.

Fig. 13.15 Start Menu

Setting up the Games Window

The first time you open the Games Explorer window you are asked if you want to use the recommended update and folder settings. If you do so Windows 7 will automatically notify you when game news or software updates are available, and will download art and information about the games on your computer, and also show when you last played a game.

You should now be ready to explore the games that are available. When you are finished with them there are plenty more to download online. Happy playing.

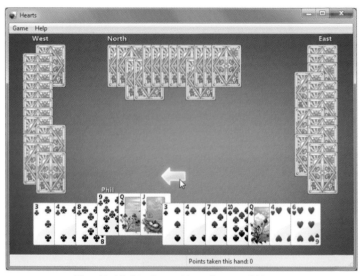

Fig. 13.16 Starting a New Game of Hearts

Appendix

Keyboard Shortcuts

Keyboard shortcuts are function keys or combinations of keystrokes that perform a command, usually without using the mouse, such as **Ctrl+C** for copy, or **Ctrl+Z** for undo.

Keyboard shortcuts are usually the most efficient way to perform commands with the keyboard, but of course you have to be able to remember them. Hence our listing here.

We suggest you browse the listings and only attempt to memorise the shortcuts that are most useful to you.

For keyboard shortcuts in which you press two or more keys at the same time, the keys to press are separated by a plus (+) sign, for example **Ctrl+P**.

General Shortcuts

F1	Display Help.
Ctrl+C	Copy the selected item.
Ctrl+X	Cut the selected item.
Ctrl+V	Paste the selected item.
Ctrl+Z	Undo an action.
Ctrl+Y	Redo an action.
Delete (or Ctrl+D)	Delete the selected item and move it to the Recycle Bin.
Shift+Delete	Delete the selected item without moving it to the Recycle Bin first.
F2	Rename the selected item.
Ctrl+⇨	Move the cursor to the beginning of the next word.

Ctrl+ ⇐	Move the cursor to the beginning of the previous word.
Ctrl+ ⇓	Move the cursor to the beginning of the next paragraph.
Ctrl+ ⇑	Move the cursor to the beginning of the previous paragraph.
Ctrl+Shift+arrow	Select a block of text.
Shift+arrow	Select more than one item in a window or on the Desktop, or select text within a document.
Ctrl+arrow+Space	Select multiple individual items in a window or on the Desktop.
Ctrl+A	Select all items in a document or window.
F3	Search for a file or folder.
Alt+Enter	Display properties for the selected item.
Alt+F4	Close the active item, or exit the active program.
Alt+Space	Open the shortcut menu for the active window.
Ctrl+F4	Close the active document.
Alt+Tab	Switch between open items.
Ctrl+Alt+Tab	Use the arrow keys to switch between open items.
Ctrl+Mouse wheel	Change the size of icons on the Desktop.
⊞+Tab	Cycle through programs on the Taskbar by using Aero Flip 3-D.
Ctrl+⊞+Tab	Use the arrow keys to cycle through programs on the Taskbar by using Aero Flip 3-D.
Alt+Esc	Cycle through items in the order in which they were opened.
F6	Cycle through screen elements in a window or on the Desktop.
F4	Display the address bar list in Windows Explorer.

Shift+F10	Display the shortcut menu for the selected item.
Ctrl+Esc	Open the **Start** menu.
F10	Activate the menu bar in the active program.
⇒	Open the next menu to the right, or open a submenu.
⇐	Open the next menu to the left, or close a submenu.
F5 (or Ctrl+R)	Refresh the active window.
Alt+⇧	View the folder one level up in Windows Explorer.
Esc	Cancel the current task.
Ctrl+Shift+Esc	Open Task Manager.
Shift	Prevent a CD from automatically playing. (Depress the key when it is put in drive).

Windows Logo Shortcuts

The following shortcuts use the Windows logo key ⊞.

⊞	Open or close the **Start** menu.
⊞+Pause	Display the System Properties dialogue box.
⊞+D	Display the Desktop.
⊞+M	Minimise all windows.
⊞+Shift+M	Restore minimised windows to the Desktop.
⊞+E	Open Computer window.
⊞+F	Search for a file or folder.
Ctrl+⊞+F	Search for computers (when on a network).
⊞+L	Lock your computer or switch users.
⊞+R	Open the Run dialogue box.
⊞+T	Cycle through programs on the Taskbar.

⊞+number	Start the program pinned to the Taskbar in the position indicated by the number. If the program is already running, switch to that program.
Shift+⊞+number	Start a new instance of the program pinned to the Taskbar in the position indicated by the number.
Ctrl+⊞+number	Switch to the last active window of the program pinned to the Taskbar in the position indicated by the number.
Alt+⊞+number	Open the Jump List for the program pinned to the Taskbar in the position indicated by the number.
⊞+Tab	Cycle through programs on the Taskbar by using Aero Flip 3-D.
Ctrl+⊞+Tab	Use the arrow keys to cycle through programs on the Taskbar by using Aero Flip 3-D.
Ctrl+⊞+B	Switch to the program that displayed a message in the notification area.
⊞+Space	Preview the Desktop.
⊞+ ⇧	Maximise the window.
⊞+ ⇐	Maximise the window to the left side of the screen.
⊞+ ⇒	Maximise the window to the right side of the screen.
⊞+ ⇩	Minimise the window.
⊞+Home	Minimise all but the active window.
⊞+Shift+ ⇧	Stretch the window to the top and bottom of the screen.
⊞+Shift+ ⇐ or ⇒	Move a window from one monitor to another.
⊞+P	Choose a presentation display mode.
⊞+G	Cycle through gadgets.
⊞+U	Open the Ease of Access Center.
⊞+X	Open the Windows Mobility Center.

Dialogue Box Shortcuts

Ctrl+Tab	Move forward through tabs.
Ctrl+Shift+Tab	Move back through tabs.
Tab	Move forward through options.
Shift+Tab	Move back through options.
Enter	Replaces clicking the mouse for many selected commands.
Space	Select or clear the check box.
Arrow keys	Select a button if the active option is a group of option buttons.
F1	Display Help.
F4	Display the items in the active list.
Backspace	Open a folder one level up (**Save As** or **Open** dialogue boxes).

Windows Explorer Shortcuts

Use these when working with Windows Explorer windows or folders.

Ctrl+N	Open a new window.
Ctrl+W	Close the current window.
Ctrl+Shift+N	Create a new folder.
End	Display the bottom of the active window.
Home	Display the top of the active window.
F11	Maximise or minimise the active window.
Ctrl+Period (.)	Rotate a picture clockwise.
Ctrl+Comma (,)	Rotate a picture anti-clockwise.
⇐	Collapse the current selection, or select the parent folder.
Alt+Enter	Open the Properties dialogue box for the selected item.
Alt+P	Display the Preview Pane.
Alt+⇐	View the previous folder.

Backspace	View the previous folder.
⇨	Display the current selection, or select the first sub-folder.
Alt+⇨	View the next folder.
Alt+⇧	View the parent folder.
Ctrl+Shift+E	Display all folders above the selected folder.
Ctrl+Mouse wheel	Change the size and appearance of file and folder icons.
Alt+D	Select the Address bar.
Ctrl+E, or	Select the Search box.
Ctrl+F	Select the Search box.

Taskbar Shortcuts

These keyboard shortcuts work when items on the Taskbar are clicked.

Shift+Click	Open a program or quickly open another instance of a program.
Ctrl+Shift+Click	Open a program as an administrator.
Shift+Right-click	Show the window menu for the program.
Shift+Right-click	Show the window menu for the group (with a grouped Taskbar button).
Ctrl+Click	Cycle through the windows of the group.

Windows Help Shortcuts

Use these keyboard shortcuts when working with the Help viewer.

Alt+C	Display the Table of Contents.
Alt+N	Display the Connection Settings menu.
F10	Display the Options menu.
Alt+⇦	Move back to the previously viewed topic.

Alt+⇒	Move forward to the next (previously viewed) topic.
Alt+A	Display the customer support page.
Alt+Home	Display the Help and Support Home page.
Home	Move to the beginning of a topic.
End	Move to the end of a topic.
Ctrl+F	Search the current topic.
Ctrl+P	Print a topic.
F3	Move the cursor to the Search box.

Magnifier Shortcuts

⊞+(+) or(-)	Zoom in or out.
Ctrl+Alt+Space	Preview the Desktop in full-screen mode.
Ctrl+Alt+F	Switch to full-screen mode.
Ctrl+Alt+L	Switch to lens mode.
Ctrl+Alt+D	Switch to docked mode.
Ctrl+Alt+I	Invert colours.
Ctrl+Alt+arrow	Pan in the direction of the arrow.
Ctrl+Alt+R	Resize the lens.
⊞+ Esc	Exit Magnifier.

Ease of Access Shortcuts

These keyboard shortcuts can help make your computer much easier to use.

⊞+U	Open Ease of Access Center.
Right Shift for 8 seconds	Turn Filter Keys on and off.
Left Alt+Left Shift+PrtScn	Turn High Contrast on or off.
Left Alt+Left Shift+Num Lock	Turn Mouse Keys on or off.
Shift five times	Turn Sticky Keys on or off.
Num Lock for five seconds	Turn Toggle Keys on or off.

Calculator Shortcuts

These are some of the more general keyboard shortcuts for working with the Calculator.

Alt+1	Switch to Standard mode.
Alt+2	Switch to Scientific mode.
Alt+3	Switch to Programmer mode.
Alt+4	Switch to Statistics mode.
Ctrl+E	Open date calculations.
Ctrl+H	Turn calculation history on or off.
Ctrl+U	Open unit conversion.
Alt+C	Calculate or solve date calculations and worksheets.
F1	Open Calculator Help.
Ctrl+Q	Press the M- button.
Ctrl+P	Press the M+ button.
Ctrl+M	Press the MS button.
Ctrl+R	Press the MR button.
Ctrl+L	Press the MC button.
F9	Press the +/– button.
Esc	Press the C button.
Del	Press the CE button.
Ctrl+Shift+D	Clear the calculation history.
F2	Edit the calculation history.
⇑	Navigate up in the calculation history.
⇓	Navigate down in the calculation history.
Esc	Cancel editing the calculation history.
Enter	Recalculate the calculation history after editing.
F3	Select Degrees in Scientific mode.
F4	Select Radians in Scientific mode.
F5	Select Grads in Scientific mode.

Index